DATE DUE		
2 6 FEB 2003		
- 6 APR 2003		
- 9 MAR 2004		
2 2 FEB 2005		
2 5 APR 2005		

2

Motivational Theories & Applications for Managers

Donald Sanzotta

Motivational Theories & Applications for Managers

amacom a Division of
American Management Associations

Library of Congress Cataloging in Publication Data

Sanzotta, Donald.
    Motivational theories & applications for
managers.

    Includes index.
    1. Employee morale. 2. Motivation (Psychology)
3. Personnel management. I. Title.
HF5549.5.M6S27   658.31'4   76-41732
ISBN 0-8144-5430-5

©1977 AMACOM
A division of American Management Associations, New York.
All rights reserved. Printed in the United States of America.

First Printing

Preface

THIS is a basic book on motivation and human behavior. It represents both a challenge and a reconciliation in explaining the principles of behavior. It will question many basic assumptions about motivation and also offer guidelines to evaluate the many diverse theories in this field.

The book is divided into two parts: theory and practice. I know many managers become impatient with theory, and many academicians cannot relate to practice, but both serve worthwhile functions and should be interdependent, and this is my approach here.

I have tried to present a flexible set of concepts for the managerial tool kit. Thus, the ideas in this kit should be more representative of adjustable, rather than box-end, wrenches. I have also tried to keep the ideas general enough to apply in a variety of organizational settings.

Most of the material for this book has come from my teaching efforts in industrial psychology, as well as from consulting assignments in the real world of business.

I owe a great deal of my experience, accumulated over the last few years, to David Ryan and Marcia Horr of the General Management Division of the American Management Associations. I would also like to thank my department chairman, Clifford Grazier, and the President of Cayuga County Community College, Dr. Albert Skinner, who have encouraged my participation in organizational consulting. Finally, I owe a large measure of thanks to Barbara Cornell, who typed the manuscript.

Donald Sanzotta

Contents

part one
Theory

1
Introduction: Why Motivation?

The Problem

Every manager talks about motivation, and there is never a shortage of opinions expressing the need for motivated workers. Further, many management scientists maintain that a motivational crisis exists in America, and some believe it is widespread and growing. Many of the facts support such a position. A new title and specialty have even emerged from this need and crisis: vice president of human resources. Organizations have spent large sums of money on human resource development programs in response to what they see as the effects of a dissatisfied, poorly motivated workforce: low productivity, high turnover, absenteeism, and counterproductive behavior.

Recently, the chairman of General Motors estimated that absenteeism on Monday or Friday company-wide had been as high as 13 percent, and for the last several years, general labor productivity has been declining at an average rate of 2 percent a year. In response to this kind of data, Senator Edward Kennedy in 1972 proposed a Worker Alienation Bill, which would set up an investigation of poor motivation and productivity and seek to counteract the problem. His proposal prompted the Secretary of Health, Education and Welfare to commission a special task force to study the situation. The report of the task force to the Secretary was published as *Work in America*.[1]

The report maintains that the average worker is bored, dissatisfied, and dehumanized as a result of organizational life. It contends that, given current trends of worker age and education, the problem will expand even further. Of the 90 million people employed today, 24 million are under 30 years old. In the next decade there will be 10 million college graduates with bachelor's degrees and 350,000 new Ph.D.'s. Assuming present employment growth rates, this amounts to two and a half graduates for every new college-level job. The implications are clear. Many new workers are going to be underemployed; that is, they will be in positions for which they are overqualified, and their lack of motivation will have all of the usual bad effects.

The importance of these problems should not be underestimated. Low productivity can have an economic ripple effect throughout our society. There are numerous examples of counterproductive behavior as a result of boredom, such as this one from an automobile assembly line: A crane operator had the job of moving a car from one subassembly line to another. The cars were lifted about 30 feet in the air, requiring the crane operator to move three or four levers. The job was dull and routine, so occasionally, to break up the day, the operator would intentionally let a car drop the 30 feet. The car would of course be demolished, and it would take 25 to 40 minutes for the parts to be collected. During that time the operator could

[1]Cambridge, Mass., M.I.T. Press, 1973.

relax, smoke, and watch the collection process. As long as this didn't occur too frequently, it was considered accidental or the result of equipment failure.

The implications of such counterproductive incidents go beyond the loss of production time or the cost of the car to the manufacturer. The crane operator doesn't pay for the damage, and the company doesn't absorb the cost increase. Eventually, the cost is passed on to the individual who purchases the car. The net effect then is that you and I pay the price of that crane operator's boredom.

Multiply this incident by the thousands of similar cases of low productivity and counterproductivity and the economic costs become highly significant. Certainly, this is not a problem restricted to the auto industry, nor even to the assembly line. Only 2 percent of the entire workforce is directly concerned with assembly line production, and 60 percent is not even in manufacturing but in service organizations.

Many organizations began to realize that the costs of low motivation and dissatisfaction needed to be accounted for and analyzed. Human resource accounting specialists are a growing segment within financial management departments. One company originally estimated the turnover costs of a manager at an arbitrary figure of $1,500. After a detailed cost analysis, the figure was revised to $12,000. Whatever was affecting turnover was also significantly affecting the operating costs of this organization.

In addition, the costs of low motivation and dissatisfaction are not only organizational, they are also personal, as illustrated by these excerpts from *Work in America*:

> In an impressive 15-year study of aging, the strongest predictor of longevity was work satisfaction. The second best predictor was overall happiness. These two socio-psychological measures predicted longevity better than a rating by an examining physician of physical functioning, or a measure of the use of tobacco, or genetic inheritance [p. 77]. Why is job satisfaction perhaps one of the best ways of ex-

tending the length of life? . . . Research findings suggest that (physical) factors may account for only about 25% of the risk factors in heart disease, the major cause of death. That is, if cholesterol, blood pressure, smoking, glucose level, serum uric acid, and so forth, were perfectly controlled, only about one-fourth of coronary heart disease could be controlled. Although research on this problem has not led to conclusive answers, it appears that work role, work conditions, and other social factors may contribute heavily to this unexplained 75% of risk factors [p. 79].

There are, of course, a complex variety of factors contributing to a motivational crisis in this country. Two general structural considerations are the large corporation and the educational system.

The birth of the large multinational corporation has created an organizational entity of enormous power and potential. In 1974, Exxon had gross sales of over $41 billion, financial resources that easily surpass the operating budgets of many countries. When a number of such corporations exist, they have a considerable economic impact. Today 3 percent of the companies in the United States employ over 50 percent of the workforce. Size on this scale also requires organizational structures designed to direct these very large labor forces toward common objectives. This often results in homogenized jobs, inflexibility on the part of the organization, and failure to address itself to the needs of the people. Such conditions lead to isolation, dehumanization, and role identity, which in turn affect motivation.

Given the size and autonomy of the giant corporation, it is possible for many managers to lose sight of the fact that organizations are created to serve people and not the other way around. Some leaders, however, are sensitive to individual differences within large organizational structures. For instance, C. Peter McColough, chairman of Xerox Corporation, has addressed this problem:

With acquisition and technology, big business is getting bigger. I think it's a real problem: How do you get a hundred thousand people or two hundred thousand people to relate? And you want them to relate not only to the smaller units, but also to the broad objectives of the corporation.

You have to strive for a new type of loyalty. . . . If they can relate and tie in their own objectives, then we have a far greater loyalty than the blind variety that many people felt toward corporations in the past. I think blind loyalty is dead.

To command the right kind of loyalty you have to make the needs of the people paramount, not the needs of the organization. If you can meet the needs of the people, you will indeed meet the needs of the organization.[2]

While many organizational leaders want to respond to the needs of their people, this is often made more difficult by the similarity of large organizations. For the individual, each large corporation begins to look like every other large corporation. Thus, the old saying "If you don't like the job, quit" is no longer a real option if it means transferring to another corporate structure. The person becomes locked in. One author maintains that the option to quit is as valid as telling a monkey in the zoo that if it doesn't like its bananas, it should go back to the jungle.

The second general structural consideration contributing to problems of motivation is our educational system. Eighty percent of the workforce in the year 2000 is on the job now or still in school. Thus, what happens within the educational environment affects the work environment for decades to come. The effect of the educational setting goes beyond the problem of underemployment and specialization (educating more people to do less) mentioned earlier. For children, school is the first organization, outside the family, in which they have a major role. How that organization is designed and how it functions can have profound and lasting effects on the personality of the child.

[2]*Xerox World*, January 22, 1971.

Within the past ten years the trend in education has been clearly in the direction of the open, democratic-style classroom. Techniques for developing autonomy, freedom, and creativity have been encouraged. Educational reformers have sent their students out as new teachers, and the result has been a transformation of the traditional classroom into a learning laboratory for the students.

What happens when these young people carry these new patterns of behavior into a job that is inflexible, boring, and unenriched? Unless our organizations can respond, we will have an ever-widening motivational crisis that will produce a population of either corporate dropouts or corporate zombies. To some extent, this is already occurring, but the present generation represents only the fringe of what is yet to enter the workforce.

Organizations are beginning to respond. Literally thousands of enterprises, both private and public, have spent large sums on motivational training, participative management programs, organizational development, and job enrichment projects. Efforts to increase motivation and efficiency have even gone into personal awareness dimensions such as sensitivity training, transcendental meditation, transactional analysis, and biofeedback conditioning.

Unfortunately, many advocates of motivational development programs momentarily take on such almost fanatical zeal that the programs become solutions in search of a problem. It seems that each new technique is *the* answer. To understand and implement each new approach would qualify the dedicated participant for a technique-of-the-month club membership. While each new or different approach has merit, it is often only a partial answer offered in relative isolation from the entire environmental problem. This leads to oversimplification and reductionism, discrediting whatever possible benefits the program may have offered.

To deal effectively with human behavior problems, managers must avoid two critical conceptual pitfalls: fragmentation and false assumptions. Fragmentation leads to inflexible, simplified cookbook decisions; false assumptions lead to wrong decisions on the wrong problems. Both types of error misguide managers and waste time, money, and resources. Unfortunately, many behavioral scientists have perpetuated such misguided efforts. Commercial motivation programs sold as commodities have led many managements down the garden path to nowhere. Too many motivation handbooks have pounds of pulp—and ounces of information. Some of the generalizations are so devoid of foundation that they could only be described as wild. None of these commercial motivation "experts" has ever adequately described motivation to me.

Just what is motivation? Every manager believes he knows something about how to motivate people. Psychologists cite studies on motivation, managers want it, students want it, housewives need it, children develop it, and yet nobody can explain it. How does motivation develop and how does it operate? Many failures to use motivation properly stem from one important oversight on the part of most managers: *You cannot use motivation properly if you don't know what it is.*

Many managers think they understand the concept of motivation, but a simple illustration will show that most people become confused easily when trying to separate motivation from other concepts of behavior. What is the difference between motivation and manipulation? Most managers respond by saying something like, "If people are motivated, they want to do something; if they're manipulated, they are forced to do something they don't want to do." This may at first sound like a plausible explanation, but it really defines nothing. Suppose I tell an assistant that if he will go to the mailroom and make me 20 copies of this page, I'll give him five dollars. Is that motivation or manipulation? What if instead I tell him that he always does such a fine job, making copies in such a fast and efficient manner, that I'd like him to make 20 more. Is that motivation or manipulation?

Usually at this point in a discussion, many people are confused by their own answers. This simple distinction is deceptively complex, and that is why the need to understand the concept of motivation becomes an imperative first step. How can we even begin to talk about management development and other complicated strategies if we can't even identify the techniques we might use to send someone on a simple errand?

To analyze the typical response stated above concerning motivation and manipulation, let us refer to those two critical conceptual pitfalls, fragmentation and false assumptions. Firstly, the answer that "a motivated person wants to do something" is circular reasoning. If he wants to do it, then he is motivated, and if he is motivated, he wants to do it. This assumes that "wanting" is the first step in directing behavior, which is clearly a false assumption. What causes the individual to want to do it? is a more fundamental question.

Secondly, the answer is fragmented into a division between voluntary and involuntary actions. Such a position ignores the interaction of motivation and manipulation. Of course, the real trap here lies not with the answer, but with the question itself. It assumes a difference exists between the two concepts. On what basis? What about the value judgments of the two terms? Would the distinction explain anything anyway? These questions must be asked first, or else, as we have seen, we end up answering the wrong question with a cookbook answer that is also wrong.

Toward a Technology of Behavior

What is the answer to the problem of motivation? If we acknowledge that motivational problems exist in our organizations, and that the manager is an easy target for misconceptions and myths about motivation, what approach should be taken?

I believe that the trends toward alienation and dissatisfaction of the American workforce can be changed, and that the leadership can be developed to do the job. The very first step is to educate the manager toward understanding human behavior. Organizations must then develop goals and objectives for human performance. The third step is to apply the principles in the form of techniques and methods to achieve the desired results. While this must be done one step at a time, the danger of fragmented and partial development, which has occurred in the past, must be avoided. We must develop a system of understanding and directing human behavior. This system must have a definite methodology and a sound theory to back it up. It must be a *technology*, as the psychologist B. F. Skinner has pointed out: "Almost all our major problems involve human behavior, and they cannot be solved by physical and biological technology alone. What is needed is a technology of behavior.[3]

Not all behavioral scientists agree that a new technology of behavior is what is needed. For many people the term creates images of *Brave New World; 1984;* and *A Clockwork Orange.* They see the ideas of control and determinism as being attached to the development of behavioral technology. They question how such new power would be used and who would control it. At the same time, other behavioral scientists believe that control, power, and domination exist now in an unpredictable and often undesirable fashion. Such dangers, they argue, are not an excuse for disregarding the need for systematic planning. Their position is that if we don't plan our consequences, we will have to settle for whatever happens. They point out that trying to pass moral judgments on the effects of what we *can* control—through careful, aware planning—is far easier than trying to judge what we don't know how to control.

The argument against a technology of behavior is an old one, and is often used against attempts to conduct research in areas of potential abuse. The position is that we should never have allowed research on the atom to be conducted, and that we should stop research in areas such as genetic engineering, electrical stimulation of the brain, or psychoactive drugs. Such an attack seems off the point. The research will continue either

[3]*Beyond Freedom and Dignity,* New York, Alfred A. Knopf, 1971, p. 24.

with public awareness or covertly and without public control. Their position would have more validity if it called for *planning and organizing control systems* to lessen the risk of abuse. If we had been developing *a control technology* for atomic power at the same time we were unleashing the atom, we would have been able to deal with the dangers of potential atomic destruction better than we have up to now.

This is also the case with a technology of behavior. As the techniques for control of human behavior become refined and more exact, there should be the simultaneous development of control systems over such power. A control system asks the question, What kind of a technology of behavior should be developed? This, of course, is a critical question and is widely debated among psychologists and social scientists. The type of technology developed depends on the theoretical position of the advocate.

For our purposes, in dealing with organizations, there are basically two conceptual positions among contemporary industrial psychologists. One position advances the ideas of human relations, human potential, and the internal power of the person. This has been labeled "humanistic psychology." The second position is newer and more controversial. It advocates the development of human potential based on the ability of an organism to learn. Its principles rest on the importance of reinforcement and punishment as the shapers of learning. This has been labeled "behaviorism."

The humanistic psychologists are represented by people like Abraham Maslow, Carl Rogers, Frederick Herzberg, and Douglas McGregor. Representation of behaviorism includes B. F. Skinner, Clark Hull, and Edward Thorndike. Many managers may recognize the names in the first category, but, with the exception of B. F. Skinner, most managers are not familiar with the behaviorists and their studies of human behavior. The positions of these two groups will be made clear in later chapters, but before jumping into the fray of ideological battle, we must develop some fundamental concepts concerning motivation.

The Basic Approach

How did the idea of motivation originate and what purpose does the concept serve? We don't need to understand motivation in order to understand all types of behavior. Reflexes do not involve intentions or drives. The knee jerk or eye blink response is not under voluntary control, but whenever we wish to understand the why of more complicated goal-directed behavior, the concept of motivation comes up.

Motivation is supposed to explain behavior. In scientific terms, an explanation involves determining causality. Thus, What causes behavior to occur? is the fundamental question in all of psychology. If we can determine causes for behavior in general, and for specific situational behavior in particular, we will be able to predict, control, and understand people. This is not a modest objective by any means, given the complexity and variability of actions and environments.

Motivation is part of causality to some experts, and to others it's simply a coincidental effect. One motivational expert talks about motivation in terms of intensity and direction. "It is generally acceptable that, in explaining goal-directed behavior, one must consider both what energizes the behavior and what directs the behavior toward the goal."[4] Another psychologist has said that there is no such thing as a person who has no motivation, except someone who's dead.

While all of these positions may have some validity, they are too abstract for the manager concerned with applying whatever knowledge psychologists may have about predicting and controlling human behavior. It is possible to predict behavior without knowing what causes it. This is done by correlating relationships of one event with another. For instance, we didn't know at first that smoking *caused* cancer, but we could predict that the action of smoking had a relationship to cancer. It may actually have been that a variable other than the smoking per se caused the cancer, but for practical pur-

[4]Edward Lawler, *Motivations in Work Organizations*, Brooks/Cole Publishing, Monterey, Calif., 1973, p. 3.

poses the relationship led us to predict satisfactorily. (Subsequent experimental studies have led to causal inferences.)

In organizations, we can predict that certain rewards will lead to specific types of performance. The fact that the rewards developed as a result of a high need for achievement from early childhood is a causal inference that may not be necessary to predict the effectiveness of the rewards. If the correlation between the reward and the performance is clear, causality is academic to the manager. A technology of behavior for organizations should begin to look at effects and abandon the elusive search for causes of behavior. This is not to say that causality isn't important, but the manager cannot wait for the behavioral scientists' research to be refined. Management must manage now, so the manager should take the knowledge that is known to psychologists and use it until better information becomes available.

While there is little valid research knowledge in many areas of behavior, there is a great deal known about behavior that has not been properly presented and shared with the segments of our society that must deal with human interactions. This deficiency of sharing is particularly apparent in the field of management training. Information, not about causality, but about probabilities of relationships, exists in areas of social influence (leadership), group dynamics, interpersonal influence, adjustment, and motivation. All these fields have something to offer the management sciences, yet because of arbitrary classifications of knowledge, cross-sectional sharing has been limited. Psychology is not business, and history is not psychology, and business is not philosophy, so we all isolate ourselves in our own academic camps.

Thus, the purpose of the chapters that follow is to address directly the motivational crisis without pretending to prescribe *the* answer. To avoid the errors of reductionism leading to fragmentation and false assumptions, evaluations of individual theories have been integrated with one another. An attempt to transmit basic knowledge of human behavior will be the thrust of what is to follow. Finally, proposals for application toward a technology of behavior will be initiated.

After reading this book, you should be able to explain the concept of motivation and how it affects behavior, but if you can do it in one sentence, or even in one paragraph, you will have failed to meet the book's primary objective: *basic* understanding of human behavior. Human behavior is not *simple*. It is complex and subject to a wide variety of conditions of influence. Hopefully, exploring these delicate areas of human functioning will give you a perspective on the richness and the complexities of managing human behavior. After all, the challenge of management is not its money, its machines, or its organization, but its people.

2
A Model
of Models

THE manager needs a complete model of motivation. There have been very few attempts to assemble the wide variety of theories into a comprehensive, dynamic model. Such a model would result from a synthesis and an interaction of discrete theories. It would not simply be a summary of different approaches that hang in midair conspicuously; rather the model should interrelate all points of view.

Furthermore, a complete model would provide the manager with a frame of reference from which to evaluate the details needed to analyze specific approaches in depth. These are the objectives of the presentation that follows.

For our purposes, there can only be two general types of motivation: extrinsic and intrinsic. The distinction is quite simple: Either the motivation comes from inside the person or it comes from outside the person. This may seem condescendingly simplistic, but unless these distinctions are made from the outset, origins of motives can become confusing, particularly in considering intrinsic and extrinsic interactions, as we will do later. In addition, it will be possible to fit the various models of motivation into this intrinsic-extrinsic distinction, which we will do after first considering some fundamental principles.

The Law of Effect

What is the *most basic* general principle of human behavior and motivation? The answer to this question, of course, has been debated for some time, but one of the closest approximations to an answer came from the psychologist Edward Thorndike, who proposed the law of effect. Essentially, the law says this: Rewarding a behavior *increases* the probability that the behavior will be repeated, and punishing a behavior *decreases* the probability that the behavior will be repeated. That is, rewarding stamps in behavior, punishment stamps out behavior. The implications of such a principle are far-reaching.

Keep one important point in mind about the law of effect. The effect of rewards or punishments does not cause anything. It only increases the probability. So, the effect is a relationship that is observable, but not necessarily causal. This, you will remember from the first chapter, is consistent with the guideline of abandoning causality in favor of developing *functional observable relationships*.

The law of effect has been demonstrated on many types of organisms in a wide variety of situations to the point of universal recognition of the tremendous power of rewards and punishments over behavior. Among humans in complex organizational environments, the law still operates, but identifying and weighting the effect of the rewards and punishments are more involved than among animals in a laboratory. Applying the law raises questions such as, What type of rewards and punishments should be used? How intense should they be? and

How frequently should they occur? Also, the law of effect must be supplemented with information about how the rewards and punishments of the past affect the future among humans, who are more intelligent than simpler organisms. That is, people develop cognitive *expectations* about the future.

The Locus of Control

The effect that expectation of rewards and punishments has on personality was investigated by the psychologist Julian Rotter. His conclusions were that people develop expectations about the source of control of outcomes. He divided individuals into two personality classifications, Internals and Externals, based on their perception of this *locus of control*.

Internals are personalities who believe that their rewards and punishments are controlled by what they do. Their own actions are the determining factor in their minds. If they perform well or if they perform badly, appropriate consequences will follow.

Externals are people who believe that forces outside themselves are responsible for their rewards and punishments. Factors such as chance, luck, and powerful other people control their consequences. Sometimes the outcomes are appropriate, an External feels, but often they are not related to what he does.

To date, literally hundreds of research studies have been conducted on the two personality types. In general, the results have shown that Internals are better adjusted, have more self-control, and are more achievement oriented. Externals tend to be more flexible, and more subject to social influence through conformity. While expectations about the control of rewards and punishments, learned from experience through the operation of the law of effect, form Internal and External personality types, very few people are either total Internals or Externals. A more realistic classification would place these personality traits on a continuum with Internal traits growing stronger toward one end and External traits doing likewise toward the other. Thus, people would have Internal or External tendencies, or more of one than the other, but would not be categorized on an absolute scale.

Whether an employee is an Internal or an External may have a significant effect on performance. Internals tend to be skill oriented, while Externals are chance oriented. Under such circumstances, leadership rests with Internal personalities who have the confidence to develop and control circumstances within an organizational structure. Externals, on the other hand, often make loyal, dedicated employees, who follow directives willingly. Several recent studies indicate that Internals demonstrate a higher degree of work motivation than Externals.

Theory X and Theory Y

With the law of effect and the locus of control as a foundation, the first familiar step of our model is ready to be added. Interestingly enough, most managers actually treat people as either Internals or Externals. This is a reflection of their basic assumptions about people.

In his book *The Human Side of Enterprise,*[1] Douglas McGregor states that a manager's effectiveness is a function of such assumptions about human nature, and that his leadership behavior will be crucially affected by them. McGregor classifies the assumptions into two hygienically labeled categories, "Theory X" and "Theory Y," which he defines as follows:

Theory X

1. Management is responsible for organizing the elements of productive enterprise—money, materials, equipment, people—in the interest of economic ends.

[1]New York, McGraw-Hill, 1960.

2. With respect to people, this is a process of directing their efforts, motivating them, controlling their actions, modifying their behavior to fit the needs of the organization.

3. Without this active intervention by management, people would be passive, even resistant, to organizational needs. They must therefore be persuaded, rewarded, punished, controlled— their activities must be directed.

Theory Y

1. Management is responsible for organizing the elements of productive enterprise—money, materials, equipment, people— in the interest of economic ends.

2. People are not by nature passive or resistant to organizational needs. They have become so as a result of experience in organizations.

3. The motivation, the potential for development, the capacity for assuming responsibility, the readiness to direct behavior toward organizational goals are all present in people. Management does not put them there. It is a responsibility of management to make it possible for people to recognize and develop these human characteristics for themselves.

While McGregor wanted these two sets of assumptions to be value-free, in most of his writing he clearly favored Theory Y.

Theory X is often seen as an autocratic, close style of supervision, and Theory Y as democratic and participative. This is basically true, but don't confuse X with "hard" management and Y with "soft" management. This is a caution McGregor said he would emphasize if he were to propose the theory again. For instance, the style of a benevolent autocrat would be a soft X. On the other hand, a leader setting rigorous objectives and evaluating performance tightly could be a hard Y. So, whether the assumptions are X or Y, the styles could still be hard or soft in either case. Also, keep in mind that while the assumptions transfer easily into styles of leadership, they are not behaviors as such. The behavior is inferred from the assumptions held by the manager.

Interactions

The alert reader will note that *the locus of control is the personality equivalent of McGregor's Theory X and Theory Y.* Managers who have Theory X assumptions about their people view them as Externals, and those with Theory Y assumptions see their people as Internals.

Two questions immediately arise from this interrelationship: (1) Are the managers' assumptions and locus of control evaluation correct about their employees? and (2) Do the managers' assumptions result from the personality types of their subordinates, or do the managers select Internals or Externals depending on whether they hold Theory X or Theory Y assumptions? While such questions may not be easily answered until specific cases are analyzed, it is apparent that cross-mixing of personalities and assumptions will result in organizational friction. A manager with Theory X assumptions is in for difficulties in dealing with Internals. Conversely, Externals will not perform well under Theory Y assumptions. Too often, managers believe that Y assumptions are superior to X in every case. This is not so, as can be seen from the positive qualities of External personalities.

Understanding this interrelationship of style and person is often considered a function of personnel selection. Unfortunately, information on the specific type of personnel to select is not offered by many personnel departments. The right employee in the right job with the right boss is the formula offered, but how does a manager accomplish this ideal combination? At least in part, the manager has to be a judge of personality. (This is not to be confused with amateur psychiatry.) Managers evaluate people all the time, and giving them the tools to practice with is long overdue.

As a manager, you already know whether many of your people are Internals or Externals. Do you deal with them on both a Theory Y and Theory X basis and is the theory matched appropriately to the person?

If you're unsure of some of the personalities of your people, or are interviewing new prospective employees, ask them questions designed to detect Internal or External traits. For example, ask them which of these two statements they consider to be more valid:

1. Becoming successful is really a matter of working hard; being lucky has little or nothing to do with it.
2. Getting a good job depends on being in the right place at the right time, and knowing the right people.

Most Externals choose the second statement. It can be a simple matter for a manager to develop similar statements and to interject them skillfully in an interview. The employee's responses to such statements will help reveal his locus of control. The objective of evaluating traits is not to make the manager an expert on personality assessment. The idea is to offer certain techniques that will add to, and not replace, the personality evaluations we all make in the course of everyday interactions. I am not asking the manager to abandon common sense reactions and intuitive feeling; I am simply suggesting a supplement.

The Need for Achievement

Among the many types of rewards that can be important to the individual, self-reward must be ranked very high. Self-reward results in a state of intrinsic satisfaction. Our culture tends, at least ideally, to consider this kind of reward to be on a higher level than material rewards, considered as ends in themselves.

Intrinsic needs, self-satisfaction, and self-reward are all considered to be an essential component of the motivation to work. Many psychologists believe that people don't work for external rewards alone, and that intrinsic rewards are at least as important in accounting for the work ethic. Questions such as, Why do people work at all? or, Why are there such differences in the commitment people have toward work? have been asked by a group of industrial psychologists.

For over 20 years, David McClelland of Harvard University investigated the distinctly human phenomenon of constructive activity beyond survival requirements. He labeled this trait "need for achievement" (n Ach). Since so much investigation has been conducted regarding n Ach, salient points of McClelland's findings are summarized:

1. Individuals differ in the degree to which they find achievement a satisfying experience.
2. Individuals with a high n Ach tend to prefer the following situations and will work harder in them than individuals of low n Ach:

    Situations of moderate risk. The rationale for this is that feelings of achievement will be minimal in cases of little risk, and that achievement is not likely in cases of high risk.

    Situations where knowledge of results is provided. A person with a high achievement motive will want to know whether or not he or she has achieved.

    Situations where individual responsibility is provided. A person oriented toward achievement will want to make sure that he or she, and not somebody else, gets the credit for it.
3. Since the business entrepreneurial role has the characteristics outlined above, individuals of high need for achievement will be attracted to that role as a lifetime occupation.[2]

McClelland believes that high n Achievers value extrinsic rewards such as money only as feedback to keep score, and that the intrinsic reward of achievement satisfaction is what stimulates their work performance.

He emphasizes the importance of high n Ach in terms of the economic growth of a society, maintaining that underdeveloped countries have populations with low n Ach. However,

---

[2]Abraham Korman, *Industrial and Organizational Psychology*, Englewood Cliffs, N.J., Prentice-Hall, 1971, p. 52.

while high n Achievers are the entrepreneurial catalysts for productive activity, McClelland stresses that no organization should contain only high n Achievers. There also need to be individuals who don't take even moderate risks (accounting department), who are not concerned with responsibility (long-term assembly line workers), and who do not require an independent freewheeling environment to maximize their achievement satisfaction.

According to McClelland, the wide differences in n Ach among individuals originate early in life and result from differences in their developmental environments. Socioeconomic background is important. An overwhelming proportion of high n Achievers come from a middle-class background. They grow up in environments in which competence is expected, independence is encouraged at an earlier age, father authoritarianism is low, and mother dominance is lacking.

In further developing a dynamic model, we can see that high n Achievers will fit nicely into the Internal personality traits, and that Theory Y assumptions would be most appropriate as a managerial philosophy. Conversely, low n Achievers could be classified as Externals, and managed under Theory X assumptions.

Motivator-Hygiene Theory

One of the most extensively researched and controversial approaches to intrinsic versus extrinsic motivation and job satisfaction has been developed by the psychologist Frederick Herzberg. His ideas have been summarized as the motivator-hygiene theory. Essentially, his contention is that the factors that lead to motivation and satisfaction on the job are unrelated to those that lead to apathy and dissatisfaction. Consider the money factor, for example. Although the lack of money makes people unhappy, plenty of money would not necessarily make them happy. Herzberg believes there is some middle ground, namely "not unhappy."

At first glance this sounds like semantic gymnastics, but there is more to it than just playing with words. Deficiency of certain factors on a job leads to dissatisfaction and no motivation. These factors are called "hygiene." This term is used because it represents preventive- or maintenance-type needs such as pay, fringe benefits, and working conditions. Hygiene factors don't relate to the job directly; rather, they concern themselves with the contextual elements of work. Not fulfilling the hygiene needs will lead to dissatisfaction, Herzberg feels. However, fulfilling them will result not in satisfaction but in the achievement of a neutral point which he calls "a fair day's work." At this point there is neither an increase nor a decrease in performance as a result of motivation.

Although proper hygiene on the job does not in itself achieve satisfaction with the job, it does serve as the prerequisite for satisfaction. At this neutral point the employee is ready for those elements Herzberg calls "motivators," which deal directly with the content of the job. Included among the motivators are factors such as responsibility, opportunities for achievement, job complexity, and growth possibilities. It is the motivators that lead to job satisfaction. Figure 1 diagrams the theory.

Figure 1. Model of motivator-hygiene theory.

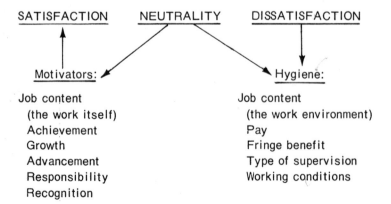

SATISFACTION   NEUTRALITY   DISSATISFACTION

Motivators: Hygiene:

Job content   Job content
  (the work itself)   (the work environment)
  Achievement   Pay
  Growth   Fringe benefit
  Advancement   Type of supervision
  Responsibility   Working conditions
  Recognition

Herzberg makes two important points in refining his theory:

1. The level of hygiene must be continually on the rise to prevent the recurrence of dissatisfaction. For instance, if a manager receives a $1,500 raise one year, and only a $500 increase the next, it's almost like getting a $1,000 cut in pay. Also, dissatisfaction will have the same effect regardless of the absolute level of needs. A vice president who feels underpaid will be as dissatisfied as a first-line supervisor who feels underpaid.

2. You don't get motivation through hygiene. Even though hygiene is a prerequisite, there will be no motivation unless you change the job. Thus, attempts at motivation through human relations, better lighting and surroundings, and increased benefits don't result in motivated employees.

According to Herzberg's approach, the only way to motivate employees is to upgrade their jobs. He has become a strong proponent of *job enrichment* as a means of tapping the motivation potential within every worker. His ideas of job enrichment, as well as the controversy surrounding the motivator-hygiene theory, will be discussed later.

Building Herzberg into our model will be relatively simple. Internal personality types would be concerned with the motivators on the job, while Externals would emphasize the hygiene factors. Theory Y managers would consider the motivators most important because they relate to job performance that is independently responsible and rewarding. Hygiene would be stressed by Theory X managers because they would feel the employee performed in response to manipulation of hygiene job factors. High n Achievers would value the motivators as opportunity, and low n Achievers would be concerned with easy work, little responsibility, and tangible extrinsic rewards.

The Hierarchy and the Model

Perhaps the most publicized theory of motivation and personality has been Abraham Maslow's hierarchy of needs. Since his approach is so generally known, our purpose here will be to restate the theory only to the degree that it will complement our model.

Maslow believed that people are concerned with satisfaction of their needs according to a system of priorities. These priorities can be divided into two general categories: *deficiency needs* and *growth needs*. Deficiency needs such as hunger, thirst, safety, and security must be satisfied before growth needs such as self-respect and self-actualization can be satisfied. Maslow felt that once a need is satisfied, it is no longer considered important, and as long as it remains satisfied, the individual will be motivated to move up the hierarchy toward satisfying other needs. Conversely, if a need is not satisfied, all the motivation of the person will be concentrated on satisfying that need to the exclusion of the higher needs. The statement "People live by bread alone when there is no bread" adequately illustrates this preoccupation with unsatisfied basic needs.

In actual situations, the transition from one level on Maslow's hierarchy to another is rather gradual. For example,

Figure 2. The traditional model.

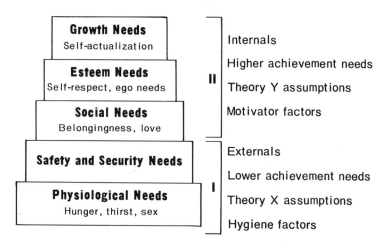

at a given time a person may have satisfied 60 percent of his security needs, 25 percent of his social needs, and 15 percent of his ego needs. The opposite, however, would not be possible, since this would violate the idea of a hierarchy of priorities.

Figure 2 represents Maslow's hierarchy as it fits into the theories discussed up to this point. The relation of Maslow's various levels and Internals–Externals, Theory X–Theory Y, need for achievement, and motivator-hygiene theory should be clear.

This completes the traditional model. While the relation of these theories to one another may be new, conceptually no new ground has been turned. Most managers are familiar with the workings of this type of model. For this reason, it will serve us well as a core of information in proceeding with the more detailed and newer areas of motivation and human behavior.

3
B.F. Skinner
& Company

Who Is B. F. Skinner?

The title of this chapter has a double meaning. Firstly, it states that the chapter deals with the theories and ideas of B. F. Skinner and his associates, the behaviorists. Secondly, it implies that the chapter will provide the foundation material for applying Skinnerian techniques in companies and organizations as a management skill.

Most managers, as one psychologist points out, are not familiar with the behaviorists:

> Since the major concern of managers of human resources is the prediction and control of behavior of organizational participants, it is curious to find that people with such a need are extremely conversant with McGregor and Maslow and

totally ignorant of Skinner. This condition is not surprising
since leading scholars in the field, of what might be termed
the applied behavioral sciences, have turned out book after
book, article after article, and anthology after anthology
with scarcely a mention of Skinner's contributions. . . .[1]

This is an interesting oversight considering that in 1971
Skinner's book *Beyond Freedom and Dignity* was on the
best-seller list for months, and that the American Psychological
Association voted him "the most influential living psychologist."

Skinner's work has, by his own admission, been slow to
catch on until recently. Nearly all of his early work was concerned with learning theory as it could be applied to animals.
The first summary of his experimental data and theory ap-
peared in 1938 in a book entitled *The Behavior of Organisms*.
During World War II, he was part of a research project that
taught pigeons, through conditioning, to peck at a screen inside
an airplane that served as an unmanned guidance system.
One reason the idea was never used was the military's concern about the effect on its image if it became known that
pigeons instead of pilots were flying our bombers. In 1948 he
wrote a novel, *Walden II*, based on a utopian society conditioned by the principles of learning theory. *Walden II* marked
the start of his concern with applying conditioning to people.

Skinner has done some controversial and peculiar experiments during his career. For example, one of his daughters
was placed in a Skinner Box from time to time instead of a
playpen. This was a climate- and germ-controlled environment
where temperature, humidity, noise, and dust were carefully
monitored. She still received the normal share of parental
attention and simply occupied this box at such times as a child
would normally be put in a playpen. The purpose of this experiment was to demonstrate (1) how children are a product
of their environmental conditioning, and (2) that greater con-

---

[1]W. Nord, "Beyond the Teaching Machine: The Neglected Area of
Operant Conditioning in the Theory and Practice of Management," *Organizational Behavior and Human Performance,* November 1969, p. 375.

trol of their environment would improve their development.
His use of the Skinner Box was not popular. Skinner also taught
pigeons to play baseball. That one took a while to live down.
The controversy surrounding B. F. Skinner, however, does
not originate with these relatively minor incidents; rather, the
storm has centered around his position of applying conditioning to society.

Despite very negative reactions to *Beyond Freedom and
Dignity*—about 80 percent of the reviews were unfavorable—
his principles of behaviorism have been adopted and applied
by many young psychologists today. These behaviorists are
not all orthodox Skinnerians, but many of the basic concepts
of Skinner are taken as core information. Often the controversy
surrounding applied behaviorism, referred to generally as "behavior modification," results from a misunderstanding of the
position and the concepts of the behaviorists. Let us then
begin with the basics.

The current belief among psychologists concerning *instincts*
is that they play an important role among animals but are
relatively insignificant among people. This leaves two major
possibilities that could affect human behavior: *genetics* and
learning. Until further research is developed and techniques
are refined, the genetic factor is not within the primary control
of the behavioral sciences. This leaves learning.

Learning in this context means *any behavior, overt or
latent, that is created, developed, or changed by the environment through experience.* This is a far-reaching definition.
Thus, understanding the principles of learning means understanding a good deal about human behavior, and this is the
conceptual position of the behaviorists.

In addition to denying the idea of instinct as an important
human behavior factor, Skinnerian behaviorists also deny the
importance of motivation. In fact, they deny that motivation
has any effect at all. Skinner describes the position:

> Instinct and drive are fictitious things put inside a person to
> explain his behavior. What we observe is that a person be-

haves in certain ways. . . . Don't look for something inside that person. If food is reinforcing, it's not because food reduces a drive, but because it has been a very good thing for the species that food has reinforced the behavior of hungry people.[2]

Among psychologists, this is a radical position, and many neo-Skinnerians and other behaviorists still rely heavily on the idea of drive, motivation, and incentive. In time, this book will develop a compromise position for the manager.

Reinforcement and Punishment

If motivation is unimportant in understanding and controlling behavior, what is important? *Reinforcement, positive and negative.* Most definitions of reinforcement follow Thorndike's law of effect in stating that an event or consequence is reinforcing if it increases or strengthens the probability of occurrence of a given behavior in the future. (This is what is meant by the term "conditioning.") If you pay a person $5 to mow your small lawn, the $5 is a reinforcer if it increases the likelihood that the lawn will be mowed again next week. This form of behavior control, because of the potential variations, is an extremely powerful tool:

> The power of reinforcement to modify human behavior is one of the most pervasive and documented findings in modern psychology; and behavior modification is the first truly effective system to harness the power of reinforcement in regulating people's actions.[3]

Every manager should understand and master the subtleties of reinforcement. Too many people have discounted the uses of reinforcement through oversimplification. As Skinner points

[2]Interview with Skinner, *Psychology Today,* November 1972.
[3]Lewis M. Andrews and Marvin Karlins, *Requiem for Democracy?* New York, Holt, Rinehart and Winston, 1971, p. 22.

out, "People get the impression that I believe that we should all get gumdrops whenever we do anything of value."[4]

Positive reinforcement is pleasant and could be considered the same as the term "reward." Negative reinforcement is not punishment. It is unpleasant just as is punishment, but it *encourages* actions that avoid the unpleasant consequences. For instance, if a rat jumps into another compartment within ten seconds after a light is turned on so it can avoid an electric shock, the shock is negative reinforcement. Actually, the reinforcement is the cessation or avoidance of the shock.

This is quite different from punishment, which is designed not to encourage action, but to *suppress* it. Suppose a rat is conditioned to press a bar to a light cue. If a shock is then introduced when the rat presses the bar, this is punishment. If negative reinforcement were being used, the rat would be shocked *unless* it pressed the bar.

This is an important difference. You don't use punishment to control what a person *should do*. You use it to control what a person *should not do*. This is the problem with punishment used alone. It doesn't direct the person into action; it simply conditions him to avoid those actions that should not be taken. By the way, an interesting effect, called "experimental neurosis," is produced in animals by punishing every action, regardless of what it is. A response of total freezing, inaction, and ambivalence occurs. This is not far removed from the effects of excessive punishment on children. Unfortunately, this freezing response to fear of punishment exists in our organizations as well.

There are two general types of reinforcement, primary and secondary. Primary reinforcements are natural and unlearned; they include food, water, sex, and most physiological satisfactions. (This, by the way, is easily associated with Maslow's first level of needs.) Secondary reinforcements are learned through a process of *association*, or *chaining*, from primary

[4]*Psychology Today*, November 1972.

reinforcements. Most reinforcements of adults in organizations are secondary; these include money, pride, achievement, and so on. This distinction will be developed further in later chapters, for it is a major point of contention between the extrinsic and intrinsic motivation specialists.

Managers can use various combinations of reinforcement and punishment. There are essentially five possibilities:

Positive reinforcement
Negative reinforcement
Punishment
Positive reinforcement/punishment
Negative reinforcement/punishment

Without going into detailed applications, examples of each will clarify the concepts considerably. If a manager rewards an employee for good performance with a pat on the back, by buying him a cup of coffee, by recognition, promotion, or money, *positive secondary reinforcement* may be operating. (We don't know for sure unless it affects subsequent performance.) If an engineer works harder to keep the boss from nagging, this would represent the effect of *negative reinforcement* (increasing a response to prevent an unpleasant consequence). If every time a personnel assistant develops a new idea, the personnel director calls it a waste of time, eventually the assistant will no longer present new ideas. This is a clear example of the effect of *punishment.* The criticism decreases—in fact, it eliminates—the response of the assistant.

Combinations are infinite in terms of application possibilities. For example, a three-day layoff for violating safety standards and a safety award for departments without a single accident for six months would be an example of *punishment combined with positive reinforcement.* Or, if a supervisor writes up a complaint on an employee for an extended lunch period, but says nothing about that employee's prompt return to work, a *punishment/negative reinforcement* strategy is being used. This suppresses the extension through punishment and reinforces punctuality through the avoidance of a reprimand. While these strategies are not new and are used by most managers, identification of just what is producing the effects often escapes the manager. This lack of understanding interferes with developing more complex and flexible reinforcement approaches.

Shaping

Why is this idea of reinforcement so important? What are the refinements needed to use it in organizations? Well, reinforcement works because of what is called the mini-max assumption. People seek to minimize pain and maximize pleasure. This is the foundation of the law of effect. This is what allows the consequences, be they painful or pleasurable, to affect behavior. B. F. Skinner develops this point further:

> Behavior is shaped and maintained by its consequences. Once this fact is recognized, we can formulate the interaction between organism and environment in a much more comprehensive way.

> There are two important results. One concerns the basic analysis. Behavior which operates upon the environment to produce consequences ("operant" behavior) can be studied by arranging environments in which specific consequences are contingent upon it. The contingencies under investigation have become steadily more complex, and one by one they are taking over the explanatory functions previously assigned to personalities, states of mind, feelings, traits of character, purposes, and intention. The second result is practical: the environment can be manipulated.[5]

As Skinner points out, consequences shape behavior. In this sense, shaping has a very specific meaning. By controlling the administration of consequences-reinforcement and punish-

[5]*Beyond Freedom and Dignity*, New York, Alfred A. Knopf, 1971, p. 18.

ment, the conditioning takes on direction. If the desired behavior is far removed from the present behavior, it must be developed gradually, and reinforced if the behavior is close to what we want. This is called *shaping*.

For instance, if we want to condition a rat to press a bar for food reinforcement in a Skinner Box, we might wait a rather long time before the bar would be pressed, since this is not something a rat normally does in a natural environment. So, to increase the efficiency of conditioning, we provide reinforcement whenever the rat comes close to the bar. (Thus it accidentally places a paw on the bar and is reinforced.) According to the law of effect, this reinforcement increases the likelihood that it will come close again. This process of shaping, also called "successive approximations," continues until the desired goal is reached.

Why do we emphasize shaping? Reinforcement will often fail if shaping techniques are ignored or if they proceed too rapidly, especially in people. Humans have all sorts of expectations, and if they feel that for any reason the reinforcements offered are too far out of reach, they will not respond for fear of failure. This fear can be minimized by using a series of steps that are reinforced and thus build on the success of past performance. You have seen this type of shaping in very basic (and often abused) form: programmed instruction.

Programming—starting with what you know and progressing with immediate feedback that serves as reinforcement—can be very effective for certain types of learning. There is one practical problem often overlooked by developers of programmed texts: As the type of learning becomes more complex, the alternative goals that may be shaped as answers must multiply to prevent dogmatic or simplistic goal direction. So for skill or technical learning, programming works very well, but for conceptual, theoretical learning, the complexity and creativity of the shaping is often lacking.

One of the most important areas of learning and behavior control is *shaping without awareness*. It is possible to shape and condition behavior without the person knowing that such shaping is operating. This phenomenon is called the Green-spoon effect.

A very simple experiment can demonstrate this effect. Holding a series of 20 three-by-five cards, the experimenter asks the subject to select at random one of three words that are on each card. The three words have different endings; for example, -ing, -ed, -tion. While the words are different on all 20 cards, these endings are the same on each card. In advance, the experimenter decided to shape the response of the subject to a particular ending, let's say -ed. When, by chance, the subject selects an -ed ending, the experimenter gives a slight nod or says "uh huh" or something similar, and says nothing when this ending is not chosen. After a number of trials, many subjects begin to respond to this subtle reinforcement by selecting the -ed ending more and more.

Interviews after such experiments have revealed that many of the subjects were not aware that the experimenter was doing anything to influence their responses. But despite their lack of awareness of the deliberate shaping, they still responded and were conditioned. The implications of the Green-spoon effect of course go way beyond this experiment. We use and respond to this effect all the time in everyday encounters. As two psychologist-coauthors point out:

> The world is, in a sense, one large "Skinner Box," or behavior control laboratory. The contents of a man's environment—his parents and friends, his house and clothing, his food and medicines, his tools and appliances—are the mechanisms by which his behavior is modified and directed. Skinner has frequently pointed out how people living together in groups consciously and unconsciously control each other's actions.[6]

This statement tends to indicate that at times the person doing the shaping may not be aware of what is actually

---

[6]Andrews and Karlins, *Requiem for Democracy?* p. 22.

happening. This can become involved. If every time an employee has a problem a manager responds by offering encouragement, who is shaping whom?

Extinction and Counterconditioning

Another principle often ignored when considering the effects of reinforcement is the absence of reinforcement. This is a kind of shaping in reverse. If we condition a rat to bar-press for food reinforcement and then no longer present the food, the bar pressing will eventually begin to decrease and will finally stop almost totally. This is called "extinction." It is not really punishment; it is simply the absence of reinforcement. Some behavior technologists advocate using a positive reinforcement/extinction combination to avoid the use of punishment and yet still suppress certain behaviors.

This positive reinforcement/extinction approach can be used by the manager in eliminating an employee's negative behavior. Suppose the manager has responded with encouragement whenever the employee came to him with a problem. The manager's encouragement (positive reinforcement) may have strengthened a dependent response and caused the employee to become overly dependent. The manager could reverse this process by using extinction, that is, by not reinforcing the dependent responses. At the same time he could reward (and thus strengthen) initiative and self-reliant behavior.

Some behavior is extinguished automatically because what is being reinforced is directly opposite of what would be extinguished or punished. For instance, relaxation is incompatible with tension and anxiety, and reinforcing relaxation serves to extinguish the latter behaviors. If being on time is reinforced, being late is automatically extinguished and promptness becomes conditioned. Being polite to customers means that the person cannot be impolite at the same time. This conditioning of opposites, called *counterconditioning*, has been used in psychotherapy for a number of years. For example, phobias, exaggerated fears, have been counterconditioned through shaping by having relaxation associated with the object or situation producing the phobia. This has been effective in as few as three or four sessions.

In management, counterconditioning is somewhat more involved. Since many seemingly opposite behaviors can be reinforced in so many ways, studying the relationships is often required. I said, for example, that promptness was incompatible with being late so that reinforcing promptness would extinguish lateness automatically. However, if being late has a more powerful reinforcement associated with it, such as a steak luncheon, the late behavior will not extinguish. Such a situation brings us to the problem of relative weights attached to reinforcement.

Satiation and Schedules

Not all reinforcement is alike. Reinforcement differs in its value to the individual, and effects will vary depending on how it is administered. Let us consider the latter situation first: administering reinforcement.

Whenever shaping toward a behavior is in process, and while behavior is reaching toward a peak frequency level, continuous reinforcement is most effective. That is, every time the behavior occurs, the reinforcement follows. This is not the most effective reinforcement strategy, however, after the behavior has been conditioned.

One of the problems with continuous reinforcement is that it is no longer reinforcing if it has been overused. For instance, if you provide continuous food reinforcement to a rat, it doesn't take very long for the rat to get full and become disinterested in the food. Satiation also applies to human secondary reinforcement, but this is more involved and will be discussed in a subsequent chapter. The point here is that continuous reinforcement is a limited tool, and variations are necessary to add practical application value to the use of reinforcement.

A partial, rather than continuous, reinforcement is known as a *schedule*. Schedules of reinforcement are based on two criteria: *time* and *responses*. A schedule based on time is referred to as an "interval schedule," and one based on responses is called a "ratio schedule." In addition, either of these two schedules can be fixed or variable, thus making a total of four basic types, each of which is designed to produce certain specific effects. The four types are:

Fixed interval. For example, reinforcement is given once every hour after the behavior has been acquired regardless of how frequent the responses are. An hourly pay rate, a weekly paycheck, or a yearly Christmas gift are all based on a fixed interval schedule.

Variable interval. For example, the hourly pay would depend upon how busy the time period was. Overtime pay and shift differentials could be variable interval schedules.

Fixed ratio. This schedule is based on performance and not time. For example, every five units produced qualifies the employee for a bonus, or every ten customers serviced earns a coffee break. Generally, incentive pay and commission sales are based on fixed ratio schedules.

Variable ratio. An example of this is an independent business venture where sometimes transactions (responses) pay off handsomely and sometimes they don't.

Of the four schedules, the most effective is the variable ratio schedule. Responses are frequent and intense since the reinforcement is never predictable but is contingent upon some behavior. One example (often cited) of its effectiveness is gambling. It is classified as a variable ratio schedule because you don't always win, and you must play in order to have a chance at the reinforcement. Simply, the variable ratio schedule lengthens the time lag between suspension of reinforcement and its identification or recognition by the subject; thus, extinction takes longer.

While in general the variable ratio schedule is most effective, the other schedules offer opportunities to fine-tune behavior. If we want certain behaviors at given time periods, the interval schedules work best. If, on the other hand, we're interested in independent performance, the ratio schedules are more useful. The fact that these various options exist should convince all managers that they have not used their imagination and ingenuity as well as they might.

Evaluating Reinforcers: Self-Report and Self-Selection

Returning to an earlier question of the value of reinforcement, how does a manager know what's reinforcing to an employee? Furthermore, how are the reinforcements ranked relatively for each individual?

Many times, managers offer rewards that they think will be reinforcing, or rewards that they have had experience with in the past. While neither of these approaches is actually wrong, they overlook one important point: A positive reinforcer is identified by its effect. If a consequence does not increase response frequency, then it is not a positive reinforcer even though it may be a pleasant event. This clarification allows us to generalize a bit and say that there are very few universal "a priori" positive reinforcers. That is, we don't really know what will function as a reinforcer for sure until we see its effect.

It is possible to get a general idea of what is positively reinforcing through a self-report questioning procedure; that is, the employee is asked what is reinforcing. Under this method two scales will result. One will be ratings *among* individuals, and the other will be relative ratings *within* a single individual. While these ratings are not a substitute for a more detailed analysis, they can form the framework for understanding what is reinforcing to your employees.

A 1974 U. S. Department of Labor study entitled *Job Satisfaction: Is There a Trend?* asked 1,500 workers to rate job

facets that were "very important" to them. Here are the top
ten rankings for both white collar and blue collar workers:

White Collar Workers	*Blue Collar Workers*
Interesting work	Good pay
Opportunity to develop special abilities	Enough help and equipment
Enough information	Job security
Enough authority	Enough information
Enough help and equipment	Interesting work
Friendly and helpful co-workers	Friendly and helpful co-workers
Opportunity to see results of work	Responsibilities clearly defined
Competent supervision	Opportunity to see results of work
Responsibilities clearly defined	Enough authority
Good pay	Competent supervision

Interestingly, in this study there were a total of 23 job factors listed, and yet with the exception of two items (opportunity to develop special abilities and job security), both white collar and blue collar workers selected the same top ten factors. So, we might conclude that reinforcers among individuals were similar. This is, of course, not the case at all. Good pay ranked tenth for white collar workers and first for blue collar workers —a considerable difference. Furthermore, within each category we are given only the average ranking, not the ranking for any one individual.

For a manager to assume that pay and interesting work have the same value for different occupational categories, or for individuals within a category, is to make random use of reinforcers, and will often result in inadvertent reinforcement of undesirable behavior. What a self-report rating does tell you, however, is the general areas of concern to the employee. This is a first step. The next step toward systematic evaluation of reinforcement is self-selection.

One widely used self-selection technique is called the reinforcement "menu." This was first used in a behavior modification classroom and consists of a list of reinforcers available. The child picks from the list based on the performance standards required for eligibility. The design and use of this approach in organizations will be developed in the chapters on application.

The Concept of Contingency

One final concept is important in rounding out this chapter, and that is *contingency*. It is probably the most important subcategory of reinforcement, and yet it is often dismissed into the ranks of jargon. Very specifically, the term "contingent" means "depends upon." Thus, we say a reinforcement depends upon a *specific* response. This is the essential difference between a pleasant consequence and a positive reinforcer. A pleasant consequence is not contingent upon a specific behavior and in turn is not a reinforcer as such. Contingency is also the essential difference, then, between successful control of reinforcement and unsuccessful manipulation. As an example, let us consider a particular aspect of contingency control.

Delay of reinforcement interferes with the association of the dependent relationship of a response and the reinforcement. The longer the delay, the less likely it is that the desired contingency of response will be attached to the reinforcement, and the more likely that "intervening behavior" will be attached to the reinforcement. For instance, if a rat bar-presses to a light cue and is given food reinforcement one minute later, it may not associate the food with the bar pressing because of the delay between the two. In addition, the behavior that occurs just before the food reinforcement will often be associated as part of the required response even though it is completely irrelevant. Thus, if during the time interval between the bar press and the offering of food, the rat turns to the left and lifts one leg, this will be incorporated in the response pattern.

The problem with delay is that it appears to the subject that the reinforcement and the behavior are not related. A gold watch given after 20 years of performance is difficult to associate with day-to-day behavior, and so is a profit sharing plan at the end of a full year. The time delay is just too long to affect short-term behavior. For this reason, immediate feedback concerning response-contingent behavior is a basic principle of successful reinforcement control.

After reading this chapter, many readers are probably feeling a bit up in the air about some of the concepts that were brushed lightly, particularly in terms of how to use these definitions, distinctions, and discoveries. Much of the information needed to apply these ideas follows, and expands and develops on this foundation.

4
Building
Bridges

Us versus Them

In Chapter 1 I asked the question, What is the difference between motivation and manipulation? My answer, at that time, was that the question was complex. Just how complex it actually is will be made clear in this chapter.

One straightforward distinction made is that motivation is essentially intrinsic while manipulation is basically extrinsic. Frederick Herzberg makes this distinction indirectly through his motivator-hygiene approach. He says that manipulation is like recharging your battery, and motivation is like having your own generator. As stated in the first chapter, such a comparison leaves a number of questions unanswered. For instance, what is recharging to your battery and what isn't? How do you get your own generator? And do batteries and generators work independently or is there an interrelationship between the two?

As a reader, you now have enough information from previous chapters to classify theorists into the two different "camps" of motivation and of manipulation if we are to use, for the present anyway, the intrinsic-extrinsic distinction. The motivation advocates would follow the well-known approaches to self-growth such as those of Herzberg, McGregor, and, of course, Maslow. The rechargers, or the manipulators, would follow reinforcement theorists such as Thorndike and Skinner.

Well then, which orientation is correct: intrinsic motivation or extrinsic behavior? The answer is that they are both right. While both are valid ways to conceptualize behavior and its potential, each looks at behavior through a fragmented and biased orientation. Thus, any complete effort to understand human behavior must take both orientations into account, and at the same time must offer a position of compromise and reconciliation that can serve as a model for managerial action.

Our approach here, as the chapter title suggests, will be to bridge the gap between intrinsic motivation and extrinsic behavior. Our method will be one of conceptually attacking and rebuilding until we have formulated a workable position for each theory. Let us begin with traditional intrinsic motivation.

The Case against Herzberg

Perhaps the most controversial theory among psychologists is Herzberg's motivator-hygiene theory. He is often criticized for his method of obtaining evidence for the two-factor theory. His original study of 200 accountants and engineers was an interview using the critical incident technique. That is, each subject was asked to recall incidents he felt satisfied or dissatisfied him about his work. After analyzing the responses, Herzberg concluded that they were grouped into two categories labeled "motivator" or "hygiene" incidents.

This method has been used to successfully replicate Herzberg's original work, but when other methods are used, his theory is not supported. There are, to date, many more studies that do not support Herzberg than studies confirming his original findings.

Bernard Bass of the University of Rochester summarizes the methodology problem:

> People are often not good judges of their own behavior. For example, nine out of ten drivers who have been objectively classified as poor drivers from their accident records feel they are good drivers. The way a person feels may not be reflected in their performance because of the tendency of individuals to rationalize their actions and feelings. It is so much easier for the individual to claim that success and positive feelings are the results of their own achievements (motivator factors) and that their dissatisfaction does not arise from their own inadequacies but is caused by another person or by environmental conditions (hygiene factors).[1]

Herzberg's theory has been attacked on grounds other than his method of gathering evidence. Some experts believe that a two-factor theory is too simplistic to address itself to the complexities of human motivation. Other criticism centers around the basic weaknesses of the theory in not explaining (1) why outcomes are attractive in terms of job factors and (2) how associations of performance, attractiveness, and job factors operate.

While all these comments must be weighted heavily against Herzberg's theory as a universal explanation of motivation, they do not destroy its core concept that there may be two dimensions influencing, on one hand, satisfaction and, on the other, dissatisfaction. The criticism does, however, dispute the notion that the job factors contributing to either satisfaction or dissatisfaction are the same for each individual, or even that

[1] Bernard M. Bass and Gerald V. Barrett, *Man, Work and Organizations,* Boston, Allyn and Bacon, 1972, p. 69.

the factors would be categorized consistently under one heading for any single person in different situations.

For example, one study conducted by Scott Myers at Texas Instruments showed that certain job factors were sources of both satisfaction and dissatisfaction. Pay was such a factor for hourly workers. This is, of course, not consistent with Herzberg's theory. Also, scientists in this study felt that responsibility problems contributed to dissatisfaction. Crossovers such as these indicate that job level, work values, age, and circumstances surrounding the work environment may change Herzberg's motivator-hygiene theory considerably, making it much more individual and general than originally proposed.

The Case against Maslow

Since many of the shortcomings of Herzberg's theory are based on the fundamental assumptions of Maslow's hierarchy, it is inevitable that we be pulled back into an examination of the arguments against Maslow. To offer managers anti-Maslow ideas is akin to high treason among Maslovian personnel and training people, but not all psychologists buy Maslow's ideas entirely.

The most basic question we can ask about Maslow's hierarchy of needs is, How valid is the order of the hierarchy? This is a devastating question in terms of finding empirical evidence to support his particular arrangement of needs, especially beyond the first two levels. Two well-recognized experts on motivation state this position as follows:

> Maslow's formulation that needs or drives are arranged in a sort of dominance hierarchy does, we think, receive at least partial support from various kinds of evidence. That the support is partial is because the evidence concerns only the needs at the two lower levels of his hierarchy, the physiological and anxiety (security) needs. . . . While there is some evidence that intense physiological and safety needs

can dominate behavior, evidence for the hierarchical relationship of other needs is wanting.[2]

Their specific points involve a number of questions concerning the hierarchy. Is it not more likely that various needs
are present and attended to simultaneously? For instance, concerns with belongingness and love are inevitably related to
self-esteem and self-respect. What happens to the hierarchy
when needs are interrelated like this? Doesn't it in effect mean
that sometimes the hierarchy applies and yet at other times it
does not?

Maslow himself acknowledged that the hierarchy was the
natural state of needs in people, but that it could be changed
through learning and cultural conditioning. Thus, people could
become preoccupied with *horizontal* movement rather than
vertical movement; that is, they could become concerned with
more and more satisfaction on the same level. When this occurs
on the lower levels, we call it materialism, a shallow development of a personality that has failed to grow in other directions.

If the hierarchy can be altered horizontally, then why can't
it be changed vertically as well? If this is possible, we have in
effect said this: The hierarchy of needs is individually deter-
mined and may have a *general* common needs arrangement
much more flexible than Maslow's representation. For instance,
the hierarchy may be divided into two broad categories, as in
Figure 3, but not generalized further.

Furthermore, we may also be required to invert or otherwise change the pyramid itself. Why? Well, what is really
meant by the statement that lower needs must first be satisfied
or gratified before moving up the hierarchy? You cannot grat-
ify certain needs out of existence. Bodily needs such as hunger
or thirst are constantly re-created. What we can assume is that
gratification means either that moderate degrees of hunger or

[2]C. N. Cofer and M. H. Appley, *Motivation: Theory and Research*,
New York, John Wiley & Sons, 1964, pp. 684, 691.

Figure 3. Maslow's hierarchy in broad categories.

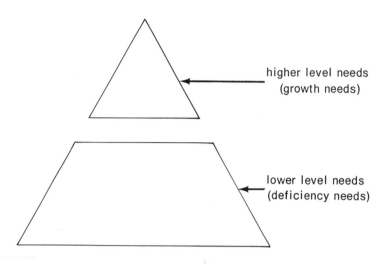

thirst are tolerated, or that a relative importance is learned in terms of what is gratification to each individual.

This last position, of course, relates to horizontal emphasis. Suppose we ask the question, Is it easier to satisfy the higher level needs in an industrialized society or in an economically undeveloped country such as India? Often, our first response is that an industrialized society provides more opportunities for satisfying higher needs because people have a better chance of satisfying the lower needs within such a system and thus have a head start. However, consideration of the horizontal phenomenon may indicate that while it is easier for people in an industrialized society to satisfy the lower needs, they can become stuck at this particular level and never reach the higher levels at all. This means that Maslow's pyramid could look like Figure 4 in terms of needs satisfied.

It is also possible that the relative perception of needs that causes this horizontal movement could reverse itself, as it apparently does among various religious men of India. They become totally unconcerned with the lower needs and preoc-

Figure 4. Horizontal movement.

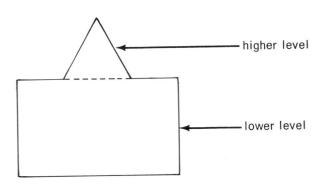

cupied with satisfying the higher levels of consciousness. In such a case, the hierarchy would actually be reversed in terms of needs satisfied and would look like Figure 5.

All of these possibilities cast Maslow's hierarchy in a completely different light. Just as with Herzberg's theory, general categories are acceptable, but specific job factors, or in this case, specific arrangements of needs, are not supported by the

Figure 5. A reversal.

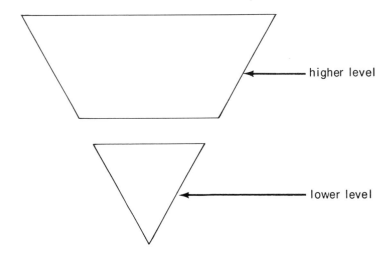

evidence of actual human behavior. In addition, if your hierarchy is not the same as mine, it is misleading to develop a model that tries to incorporate both sets of needs. Wouldn't it be better to inductively evaluate each individual's hierarchy and then offer several general models that are flexible and in turn more realistic and useful?

This, by the way, is exactly what Maslow had in mind. After studying the major theories of personality and the religions of the world, he came up with this hierarchy, but he meant it to be only a general framework, not the plug-in cookbook model that managers have made of it. So don't blame Maslow if your people don't line up with the categories. These are the needs that people as a whole are concerned with, but they are based on an individual emphasis and a concurrent interrelatedness of one need to another.

Reinterpreting Herzberg and Maslow

Is it possible to reinterpret Herzberg and Maslow through the behavioristic extrinsic motivation model? If we can present a consistently related picture to the manager, it follows that it will be easier (and more effective) to apply these various theories.

In Chapter 3 we noted that continuous reinforcement is best when a behavior is in an acquisition stage, but after it has become conditioned a partial schedule is most effective. This is due, in part, to the fact that a satiation effect occurs faster on a continuous schedule than on a partial schedule. Well, just as schedules influence satiation, *certain types of needs are more easily satiated than others.*

For most people, satisfying a hunger drive is considerably easier than satisfying a need for self-esteem. A tangible primary reinforcement is involved in one, while an intangible set of conditions (secondary reinforcements) prevail in the other. In fact, we may extend ourselves a bit and say that, in general, a primary reinforcement satiates (a lower level need)

Figure 6. Conversion of motivator-hygiene factors.

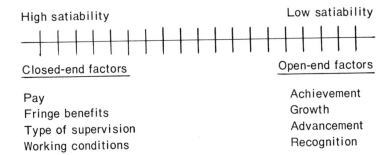

High satiability

Low satiability

Closed-end factors

Open-end factors

Pay
Fringe benefits
Type of supervision
Working conditions

Achievement
Growth
Advancement
Recognition

more easily than a secondary reinforcement satiates (a higher level need). At the same time, though, we cannot deny the maintenance nature and power of primary reinforcers. The point here is that if Herzberg's motivator-hygiene theory were viewed in a slightly different manner, it could fit into a behaviorist's model. For purposes of illustration, let us change the heading on motivator and hygiene factors as in Figure 6.

It is not unreasonable to put Herzberg's hygiene factors under the high satiability dimension and the motivator factors at the other end of the continuum of low satiability. Let us, however, interject one conditional statement to make our earlier critique consistent with this illustration. I would not place specific job factors under either the closed-end or open-end classifications, just as I would not list specific motivator or hygiene factors. Rather, satiation should be considered idiosyncratic, based on individual subjective histories and perceptions of reinforcement. A reinforcer that may have a high satiability quality for one person may be an open-end factor for another.

It should be clear that in using job factors any manager has much more flexibility with factors of low satiability than with those of high satiability. What occurs is that the former factors don't "wear out" like the highly satiable factors.

How, then, does a manager determine satiability of job factors? In two ways: functionally and predictively.

A *functional analysis* is done by using three factors:

Baseline frequency of the response.
Contingencies that follow.
Change in frequency as a result of the contingencies.

By studying these three elements *over time* you can develop a set of satiability ratings for the contingencies. If the baseline frequency is changed as a result of the reinforcement and it maintains this new level, apparently the reinforcement has not reached a satiation point. For example, if every time, and no matter how often, an employee is given praise there is a corresponding behavioral change, then praise has a low satiability quality for that person. Stated differently, a functional analysis means that a data sheet is developed based on what actually works in a particular situation.

A *predictive measure of satiability* is more difficult since it is not dealing with an after-the-fact analysis. It may take the form of a report from the employees themselves on how reinforcing they feel certain factors are, or it might be based on job level, work values, types of needs, and other indirect measures. Classifying and evaluating reinforcements is something that will be explored further in subsequent chapters.

What is really being pointed out when we discuss the types of reinforcements involved in establishing relative satiation effects is Maslow's hierarchy concept. Managers can develop a *satiation hierarchy* that would be based on the nature of the individual's needs and on the level of the need. In this way, we are calling Maslow's deficiency needs highly satiable and the growth needs open-ended or of low satiability. From this perspective, on each need level we could also develop a reinforcement hierarchy as well.

At this point, the reader may say that we are simply renaming the same old ideas. Well of course we are, but the effect of this relabeling is significant because of what the labels are based on. On one hand the labels of Herzberg and Maslow are based on assumptions of intrinsic motivation, but the new labels are based on extrinsic reinforcement. These two positions originally couldn't be further apart or more different from one another.

The Case against the Behaviorists

If the major problem with intrinsic motivation theories is the lack of empirical evidence and support, what then, in the interest of balance, is the major limitation of the extrinsic motivation concepts? The answer to such a quesion is perhaps the opposite of the answer for intrinsic motivation theories. Where the findings of intrinsic motivation advocates can't be verified because their theories are too involved and complex, those of the extrinsic motivation people can easily be verified because their approach is too simple.

The behaviorists' position is basically flawed by the simplistic interpretation of their model. This is partly inherent in the model itself, but it is mostly the result of improper or at best misleading interpretations and inferences. Since a great deal of the work in behaviorism over the last 50 years was conducted using animals, many of the initial inferences concerning applications to human behavior either were wrong or didn't go far enough to explain the complexities of such behavior.

Maslow summarizes this position well in his book *The Psychology of Science*: "I believe mechanistic science (which in psychology takes the form of behaviorism) to be not incorrect but rather too narrow and limited to serve as a general comprehensive philosophy."[3] Behaviorism is correct as far as it goes, but that it doesn't go far enough is the constant message coming from the intrinsic motivation people.

It is clear from experience with people that in order for behavior to occur there does not always have to be a "gumdrop"—a reinforcement that is directly related. Sometimes behavior is not reinforced for long periods of time. Some individuals will work years for economic success, academic de-

[3]New York, Harper & Row, 1966, p. 176.

grees, or recognition without any significant tangible reinforcements. According to the behaviorist principles of Chapter 3, the behavior should soon extinguish itself in the absence of reinforcement, or, even more likely, competing behavior that is reinforced should take over in place of the unreinforced behavior. And what about the growth needs of a person? How are they developed without direct tangible reinforcement?

These issues had to be addressed by the behaviorists in order to carry their approach beyond Pavlovian conditioning or simple stimulus-response associations. One of the first major attempts to add a motivational aspect to conditioning was Clark Hull's work. Hull maintained that there were basically three factors controlling responses or behavior:

Drive. This has an energizing influence as a result of deprivation.

Habit. This gives the drive direction and is the connection between the stimulus and the response that is built up through reinforcement.

Incentive. This adds the element of expectation to behavior, through the anticipation of a goal.

According to Hull these three concepts are interrelated, and their relationship can be described in the following formula:

$$\text{Behavior strength} = \text{drive} \times \text{habit} \times \text{incentive}$$

This is the first step toward a compromise position between the strict Skinnerians (reinforcement) and the intrinsic Maslovians, but it is only a tentative position since it relies mainly on external secondary reinforcement. *In order for an incentive to develop through habit, there must be a reinforcement to reduce drive.* So, to at least some degree we're still in the same position of weighing extrinsic reinforcement as a crucial variable even though we have added some additional elements to account for more complex behavior. Two experiments will illustrate this point further.

Experiment 1. Psychologists can easily train a chimpanzee to insert poker chips into a vending machine in order to receive a grape as food reinforcement. The chimp is then required to learn to use another machine to get the poker chips. If the animal is prevented from "spending" the chips immediately, it will still collect them, engaging in a kind of hoarding, or amassing of "wealth."

This is a fairly complex set of secondary reinforcers: the poker chips, the chip machine, and the storing up of potential reinforcement. At one time the behaviorists believed that this type of chaining could account for all types of behavior, however complex, but the second experiment creates a bit of a problem for this model.

Experiment 2. Psychologists have recently been reinvestigating an area that had been ignored for many years—the idea that a basic exploratory or curiosity drive may be present in all animals. The hypothesis is that such a basic drive or motive would seek out stimulation and perhaps even seeks challenge.

Suppose some nuts are placed inside a chest that a chimpanzee can open by manipulating a set of levers and catches. A chimp in this setting of course will work for the reinforcement, as we might expect. But what if, at the same time, nuts of the same type are placed right next to the chest, where they are available freely and easily? The chimp will still work the levers and eat the nuts in the chest, ignoring, or only incidentally regarding, the nuts that require no effort at all to obtain. Why? What is the reinforcement?

In the first experiment the hoarding behavior will continue only if the chimp can use the poker chips at least *sometimes* to get a food reinforcement, but in the second experiment the chimp will manipulate the levers even if there are no nuts in the chest, or even if there have *never* been any in there. Thus, in the first instance the behavior suffers "experimental extinction," but in the second case it is not extinguished. Why this difference, and why has it been overlooked for so long (this second experiment was first conducted in 1881)?

Some behavior may have no visible association with primary or even secondary extrinsic reinforcement. For instance, we don't stop saving money because it isn't translated into "grapes," we don't lose interest in music simply because our parents are no longer offering positive or negative reinforcement, and some workers don't lose their drive for working even though they no longer receive substantial pay increases. The answer offered by the behaviorists as well as the intrinsic motivation people is that some kind of self-reinforcement is operating. Well, what kind? And how did it get to be intrinsic?

The Bridge: Functional Autonomy

In trying to answer these questions, I came across the work of Gordon Allport, originally published in the 1930s and revised in 1961. He was a personality theorist and would not like to be associated with the behaviorists, but he might not mind having some of his work represent a middle position in this extrinsic-intrinsic motivation controversy. I have adapted many of his ideas to form a compromise position for the manager. Many of the hypotheses that follow are tentative and subject to modification after meeting the tests of continued application.

Although we have now reached the point where we acknowledge two separate types of motivation—extrinsic and intrinsic—we still need an essential link between the two, and Allport's work helps to provide that link. A simple case may help to conceptualize the situation. Our setting is the 1950s in a lower socioeconomic environment, and a 15-year-old boy is our main character. This boy feels a tremendous deprivation and an equally strong need to be economically secure. As a result, he takes a part-time job after school and saves the bulk of his pay. After high school, he takes evening college courses and works full-time. In a short while, he has saved enough money to start a small business of his own. Since his investment is small and the risks of failure are large, he works very long hours. He gets up at 6 o'clock, is at work by 6:30, and doesn't leave until late in the evening.

With the combination of hard work, a good business, and considerable luck, the business begins to thrive. In time he has a large home, a yacht, an airplane—all the material things he could want. He is economically secure. At this point, we might expect him to work at a much less rigorous pace, but he doesn't. He still gets up early and still spends long hours at work. He may even do this to the point of risking his health.

If we asked him why he maintains such an exhausting schedule, he would say, "I just get a kick out of doing it" or "I like to keep my hands on what's going on."

How does reinforcement theory explain this? Well, we're now concerned with what we'll call the *transformation of motives*. What has happened is that the original motive of our subject—to work hard as a means to the end of raising his socioeconomic status—has been transformed into an end in itself. That is, in this process, *means* become *ends*. Allport describes this as follows:

> In all cases the activity that later became motivational was at first instrumental to some other end (i.e., to some earlier motive). What was once extrinsic and instrumental becomes intrinsic and impelling. The activity once served a drive or some simple need; it now serves itself.[4]

This kind of internalizing can involve the pursuit of literature, clothes, workmanship, or challenge. All of these pursuits may have once served to obtain outside reinforcement, but now they become interests in themselves. This may sound like secondary reinforcement, but it is not, because the motives separate themselves even from secondary associations.

This separation is called *functional autonomy*, and the term describes the concept. As used here, the word "functional" means that the motives serve a present need, not a need of the past: "... past motives explain nothing unless they are also present motives. ... As the individual (or the motive) matures, the bond with the past is broken. The tie is functional, not historical."[5]

[4]*Pattern and Growth in Personality,* New York, Holt, Rinehart and Winston, 1961, p. 229.
[5]Ibid., p. 21.

The term "autonomous" deals with this breaking-off of motives: To the extent that a present motive seeks new goals, it is functionally autonomous. "Functional autonomy," then, refers to any acquired system of motivation in which the tensions involved are different from the tensions from which the system originally developed.[6]

What functional autonomy is all about is the transformation of behavior that is rewarded externally into behavior that is self-rewarded. This represents a critical step that is missing from our model in Chapter 2. The functional autonomy process bridges the difference between Theory X and Theory Y, Internals and Externals, high and low need for achievement, and motivator and hygiene factors. In general, on the lower levels the motives in Maslow's hierarchy are not functionally autonomous, while on the higher levels this transformation has occurred. However, we must realize that the possibility exists that any motive, even those in the lower levels, can be transformed.

Managing Autonomy

What does functional autonomy mean to the manager? Depending on circumstances, a manager may or may not want to have people with functionally autonomous motives. The challenge to management, then, is threefold: determining (1) what motives should be autonomous, (2) how they are identified, and (3) how to condition for autonomy. While it is the task of the following chapters to address these three points, one final comment is appropriate.

It is possible to condition functional autonomy in two directions—from extrinsic to intrinsic, or the *reverse*. Again, a vignette will serve as a useful example:

There was an old man who lived alone in a house on a street filled with children. The children liked to play right in

6Ibid., p. 22.

front of the old man's house, always making a great deal of annoying noise. The man decided to do something about this (functionally autonomous) behavior. On Monday he called the children inside and told them how much a lonely old man like himself enjoyed children playing and making noise in front of his house. He enjoyed it so much that he would give each of them a quarter if they would do the same thing the next day.

On Tuesday the children came to the old man's house and made a heck of a racket. Afterward they each received their quarter, and he asked them to come back and play tomorrow, but since he was not wealthy, this time he could only afford 15 cents for each of them.

On Wednesday the routine was repeated, except that the man said he could afford only five cents for Thursday. At this, the children were quite annoyed and said they wouldn't bother to play in front of his house for just a nickel. Whether he realized it in our technical terms or not, the old man had succeeded in extrinsically reinforcing the children's functionally autonomous behavior and then extinguishing it.

5
Redefining Motivation

MANAGERS' ideas about motivation often rest on opposite ends of a balance scale. On one end are the managers who feel that human motivation is too complex to be understood or, if it can be understood, that it's impossible to change most people anyway. I call these managers the *determinists*. On the other end of the scale are the managers who believe that motivation is something that you give to or take away from a person as though it were some sort of commodity. I call these managers the *manipulators*. Exploring the truths and myths of each position may help us to develop a better and more workable concept of motivation for managers.

The Determinists

Managers on this end of the scale identify with what psychologists call the "black box problem." The problem rests on the assumption that in terms of attitudes, motives, thoughts, and insights the human mind is inaccessible to outsiders and thus is a mystery. Trying to "see" a person's motives is like looking into a black box.

This point of view may sound like that of the behaviorists, who do not make inferences about internal processes, and it is to a degree. The difference comes when we compare the conclusions of the deterministic managers with those of the behaviorists. The determinist philosophy is that the black box is a tangle of confusion, and only those motives which are shallow and superficial are worth dealing with. Behaviorist assumptions, on the other hand, center around the idea that the black box is not worth dealing with because it's empty, and the richness of human life lies in the understanding of outward behavior.

The determinists' assumptions lead them to adopt a strategy of partial resignation, which says in effect, "We'll never really understand people. I don't care what you say; people are people, and that makes them unpredictable."

Any manager who feels that way is ready to fall into the reward and punishment trap. This trap is what Harry Levinson calls "The Great Jackass Fallacy." It goes like this: If people are too complicated to understand, you have to do your best in controlling them by studying their reactions. Since the deterministic manager already assumes that you cannot go too deeply into human understanding, the "study" turns out to be very superficial, observing only the grossest reactions to extreme forms of rewards and punishments.

In short, this approach leads to the conclusion that a jackass and a person have much the same reaction to life. They both display behaviors of stubbornness, stupidity, and unwillingness to go where driven, and they both react to the carrot (reward) and the stick (punishment). In truth, people do act this way when they are dissatisfied, not motivated, or are otherwise alienated from their "controller" or their situation, but these traits are by no means a full list of human behavior. To believe that they are is to have a very superficial knowledge and awareness about people.

You know, an old story that deterministic managers love is the one where a farmer hits a jackass over the head with a two-by-four to get his attention. The point is supposed to be that you have to do this with people too. Well, that may be a cute story, and for all I know it may even be a good way to get a jackass's attention, but it's a pretty stupid way to handle people.

For the deterministic manager the choice in terms of a course of action is either to resign himself to the fact that there is nothing that can be done about human behavior, or to react with simplistic overkill. Since their managerial position does not allow complete abandonment of control, they are usually compelled toward this overkill, which takes the form of the reward and punishment way out. "If they don't fall into line, hit'em over the head until they do," or "If you give people enough money, they'll do anything."

Of course, this attitude is not wrong as such; it's just not the whole story. Unfortunately, this oversimplified approach works just enough of the time to reinforce itself and keep the deterministic manager from seeing its limitations. When it doesn't work, it's written off as a further confirmation that you can't get everything out of the black box, so you just play the averages. What these managers don't realize is that when you purposefully resign yourself to playing the averages, that's how your performance record as a manager looks—very average. There are enough situations beyond a manager's control in interpersonal relationships without his creating artificial roadblocks.

The Manipulators

Both the determinists and the manipulators have preconceived ideas about motivation, but the manipulators become more of a problem since they are more likely to actively pursue these preconceptions. A determinist will hire and fire or offer simple-minded rewards and punishments, but manipulators work out strategies to confirm their predetermined philosophies about employees' needs.

The manipulators are the first bandwagon participants whenever a new approach to motivation becomes the thing to try. They got in on the human relations movement of the 1940s. They became the participative managers of the 1950s. The 1960s saw them in T-groups, and they're in on job enrichment in the 1970s. It's too bad that they don't know a little bit more about motivation. If they did, they just might not look so foolish historically.

Their philosophy, often the opposite of the determinists', says in effect, "We really don't know what to do about the situation, but let's try this. It can't hurt." They're managers in search of a cause. They want to advocate something, any-thing, so they become prime targets for the latest cookbook recipe of pabulum. They could avoid the indigestion that this approach causes if they would accept just one principle: Moti-vation is complex but it does not defy common sense.

Perhaps the most flagrant misconception of motivation and violation of common sense is the *single motive fallacy*. As the word "fallacy" indicates, the assumption that a person has one goal or a single drive is wrong. To assume that a single type of reward or punishment determines motivation requires that we ignore the most obvious observations of everyday behavior.

For example, let's look at the most widely used form of reward in our society—money. Superficially, we might say that the motivation to work comes from a simple exchange process of trading time and effort for money. Thus, we have deter-mined a means-end relationship. This would further lead us to the conclusion that there is a ratio between time-effort and amount of pay, and increasing or decreasing one will affect the other. Clearly, this is not, in fact, the case, and for several reasons.

First of all, such an analysis ignores the common observation that money can become a habit-forming drug, independent of any time and effort input. The drive for financial gain, regardless of how it is secured, is something we all learn about very early in life. It's called "exploitation." In more objective terms, this independence of money from time and effort amounts to a breaking-down of the means-end relationship that may have once existed. In other words, money can become functionally autonomous.

Secondly, the simplicity of a time-effort/money ratio does not take into account an almost endless list of intervening variables, such as:

What other companies pay.
What other people in the company are paid.
Personal history of salary increases.
Personal goals and present expenses.
Work load and level.

The list could go on and on. Each item would change the nature of the means-end relationship.

It is possible to use any type of reward or punishment in the above analysis. Money, praise, status, layoffs, reprimands, embarrassment, or firing all have intervening variables which make the single motive approach a fallacy.

Nevertheless, the single motive fallacy is part and parcel of the manipulators' mentality. As a spin-off of this fallacy, all sorts of managerial assumptions arise—such as absolutism, condescension, and presumption—which cloud the essential role of motivation in human behavior.

Absolutism versus Relativism

Absolutism comes from our belief in universal principles, rules that apply independent of the situation. Philosophers call it "Truth." Scientists for a long time felt that we could understand these principles through the scientific method of observation, and in fact the method has taken us a long way toward that goal, but we are not there by any means. For example, if you asked me, as a psychologist, to give you *five* principles of human behavior that apply to all people, at all times, and in all situations, I couldn't do it. You might then, as some managers do, say that psychologists really don't know anything about people. This is a trap of absolutism. "If you can't tell me everything, you can't tell me anything."

In discussing principles of human motivation, we must accept a philosophy of relativism not absolutism. The characteristic of any applied discipline is that the situation determines the nature of the principles to be applied. This, again, can throw managers off guard because of the desire to use plug-in motivation principles.

In counteracting absolutism, we are faced with the problem that relativism presents, namely, matching the treatment to the ailment. This often reduces to a matter of perception. The political philosopher John Locke conducted an experiment in the early 1700s showing the connection between relativism and perception. It is one of those experiments that's so simple it's beautiful. He placed three bowls of water in front of a subject. One contained hot water, one cold water, and one warm water. The subject placed one hand in the hot water and the other in the cold water for five minutes. Then both hands were put into the bowl with warm water, and the subject was asked to determine the temperature of the water in that bowl. Of course, you know the result: The warm water felt cool to one hand and warm to the other.

Since relativism depends on where you're coming from, empathy becomes one of the best methods for understanding the perception of others. Remember, no matter how objectively you may "see" the situation of someone else, *perception determines reality* for that person. What are the implications of all this in explaining motivation?

The implications of perception and relativism center around the concept of an incentive. The word "incentive" comes from "incite," which means "to stir into action." Psychologists would call this a "stimulus." A stimulus initiates a response. However, there is a more basic question that is addressed by the study of perception. What makes a stimulus a stimulus or an incentive an incentive? After all, if the employee does not perceive what you offer as an incentive, then in fact for that person it isn't one. In turn, we have no stirring to action, no motivation.

This consideration of the role of perception calls into question the whole idea of motivation being something that you give to someone. Actually, the question, How do I motivate my people? is itself condescendingly manipulative. It assumes that you are in some sort of an elitist position—that you have something another person doesn't have but are willing to share it. This of course is nonsense. It makes motivation into a commodity. "Would you please pass the motivation to this end of the table?"

Perception makes any incentive relativistic; that is, the incentive depends on the person and the person's perception of the incentive. Thus, the manager must match the principle with the situation. This may sound simple, but it isn't at all. What we're saying is that the same technique will often produce different results for different people, or even for the same person at different times.

Overlooking this concept of relativism has led to a number of misguided efforts in an attempt to discover certain absolutes about employees. Personality testing has been one of those areas. Perhaps the single most important benefit of administering tests to employees is that it gives the personnel department something to do. It also gives them a tangible commodity to show management. This is not really personnel's fault, since the demand for absolutes comes from the managerial mentality that expects this sort of thing in the first place.

Not only can you learn how to take a personality test to score any way you choose, but the testing may evaluate traits that have no connection with the requirements of the job. Aside from those drawbacks, personality testing assumes that personality is a measurable quantity that is a constant. Once you assess a person, he stays assessed in that way.

Recently, the whole concept of personality has taken on a relativistic quality. Some psychologists now believe that personality consists of a collection of roles. These roles are determined by the individual's perception of the situation. For instance, your perceived role with your boss may be quite different from your perceived role with your employees. If we got a personality description of you from your boss and another from your employees, in some respects it would seem as though they were talking about two different people. How, then, can we say that the same incentive will work in both situations? Furthermore, these are formal roles. In one case you have the role incentive to be a follower with ideas, and in the other case your role incentive is to be a leader with ideas. When we add the variable of informal or spontaneous roles, absolutism in terms of personality is even less valid.

It follows, then, that if a person's role changes, his incentives and motives also change. These changes may be beyond your control or you may be the catalyst for the change. In either case, your acceptance of the relativism involved will keep you from falling into the abyss of the black box, and throwing your hands up in despair.

What Is Motivation?

If motivation and its attendant incentives are a matter of perception, the next question is, What are the perceptions that precede motivation? In effect, the question is, What is motivation? Again, this is a crucial first step for managers if they are to tap that productivity resource.

Just what exactly is that trigger for action? We have examined many of the theoretical positions in the preceding chapters, and their assumptions have directly, or implicitly, been stated. However, a general or overall theoretical view is our purpose here. Let us examine some of the general assumptions about motivation in an effort to arrive at a conceptual redefinition of motivation.

Motivation as Competition

People are social creatures who rely on group behavior for support and survival. Urban dwellers do not raise their own food and must therefore pay others to do it. Farmers become more efficient through the development and use of equipment manufactured by the urban dweller. In countless ways we are interdependent, and nowhere is this social interdependency more necessary than in our organizations.

Interestingly, for a variety of reasons, competition has often played a role in social interaction. Affluence can afford us leisure time that may encourage the development of sporting activity. It is no secret that the American business community places a high value on the competitive spirit. The idea of winning at the business of business is a very common feeling in the executive suite as well as on the loading dock. The games are different, the stakes often change, but the competition is there all the same.

Let's not kid ourselves about competition. It's exciting. The adrenalin it inspires may provide us with the opportunity to achieve the kind of peak experiences that are genuinely memorable. Some time ago, in talking with Jim McKay of ABC's "Wide World of Sports," I asked him what he felt was the role of competition in our society. He replied that his exposure to athletes (which has been considerable) had led him to believe that their efforts, discipline, and motivation represented the upper reaches of human achievement, and that "the thrill of victory and the agony of defeat" were very real.

Now, many students of organizational development believe that we could use, and greatly benefit from, more of that kind of motivation in our organizations. They would have us believe that competition represents a basic social drive. About their own behavior, people need to ask the question, Compared to what? in order to get the kind of feedback that is meaningful and will lead to further incentives toward a standard of excellence.

Viewed in this way, competition can be motivational. It can represent a comparative system of rewards and punishments, and, depending on the nature of the competition, it can provide immediate feedback that allows for the continuous development of newer and better responses. This feedback can serve as a built-in shaping mechanism.

From this, can we make the statement, Competition has a proper place in the definition of motivation? Yes, but with the conditional term *proper place* being significant.

The effects of the competitive mentality on motivation and business performance are readily observable. Robert Townsend's best-seller *Up The Organization* reads like the handbook for a football team. As CEO of Avis Rent-A-Car, Townsend based his advertising campaign and the company's rapid growth on the competitive spirit. "We're number two; we try harder" is the essence of comparative motivation.

However, with the idea of comparative motivation as an acceptable and workable approach, we must back up and understand the term "proper place." Competition can have two distinct disadvantages that can actually suppress motivation or render it counterproductive.

In our earlier discussion of shaping and rewards and punishments, we stated that if the perceived gap between present behavior and a particular goal was too wide, conditioning might fail. This same principle applies whenever we attempt to use competition as a motivating device. If a person perceives his present behavior and his behavior potential as very short of a goal, often a frustration and disengagement response sets in.

To avoid this problem, the level of competition should be related to the level of performance, or more precisely, it should be a *just noticeable difference* above the level of performance. Also, for competition to be an effective motivator, we must consider the locus of control from our model in Chapter 2.

There is some evidence to suggest that competition is a stronger motivator for Internals than for Externals. This makes sense if we consider that a person must first believe that competitive effort is going to make a difference in terms of the outcome. An extreme External will not accept this formula and will frequently be labeled as "a not very tough competitor."

A second disadvantage of competition as a motivator is its potential destructive effect. Competition can encourage a standard of excellence, but it can also encourage suspicion, blaming, reprisals, and other counterproductive behavior. These negative results can destroy an individual and an organization. Such negatives occur between competing individuals, departments, and companies. Managers have discussed with me on many occasions how departments defeat organizational goals through subtle competitiveness, such as withholding information or stalling on project deadlines.

Our society has encouraged competition with noble goals in mind; however, we have overlooked an important consideration. There is a major difference between destructive competition and constructive competition. Destructive competition fosters a "we-right-friendly, they-wrong-hostile" mentality. Constructive competition is collaborative and team-oriented. In our organizations, a result-focused structure can develop competition, and, again, in its proper place it has served its pragmatic purpose well.

At some point, individual competition must be balanced with group effort, and at times the two do not complement one another. Of course, the balance point depends on—you guessed it!—relative perception. How do the participants view their role and purpose in the competition? If they see their role as antagonistic, we may have destructive competition. If, on the other hand, they see their role as contributory, constructive competition may result.

Your role as a manager in this perceptual process consists of a sequence of empathy, assessment, and action. After you make an effort to understand the employee's perceptions, you can then decide a course of action based on our model. Your assessment should take into consideration the kinds of rewards and punishments that would be appropriate as well as how shaping should proceed. Considerations such as need level, degree and type of functional autonomy present, and individual goal direction must also enter into the picture.

Now that we have acknowledged a role for comparative motivation in the form of competition, we are still left with a nagging question, What makes competition attractive? That is, is there a type of motivation that is even more basic?

Motivation as an Innate Drive

In the last chapter we discussed the possibility of a basic exploratory drive. It may be of value to discuss this further to help our definition process. One of the major adaptations of many species is their flexibility. The drive to locate new sources of food and potential mates and to develop territorial "maps" for security and rapid escape all have survival value. These may be seen as direct benefits to the curious animal.

Various studies of curiosity have been conducted on animals. One such study investigated the responses of several hundred different types of mammals to novel objects introduced into their cages at a number of zoological parks. The greatest variety and amount of investigatory behavior were observed in those animals who had (1) a relatively well-developed brain, (2) good manipulative skills, and (3) relative security from predators in a natural habitat. These conditions are met by a variety of primates, such as baboons, chimpanzees, and, by the way, humans.

Other studies have indicated that this curiosity or exploratory drive in primates is related to age. Figure 7 shows this function. As you can see from the graph, both infants and mature adults show less investigatory behavior than do children and young adults. This correlates with the relative importance of early life as an optimal time for learning. The

Figure 7. Relationship of age and curiosity in primates, including humans.

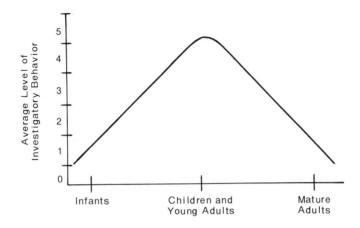

graph represents a composite trend for all primate species, including humans.

To the extent that exploration and the seeking out of novel experiences is related to motivation, we may conclude that there exists a certain built-in factor of determination for the level of drive a person feels. In explaining all motivation, however, the innate drive approach falls short. It does not address itself well to the development of more complex forms of motivation. There is no direct translation process in which an exploratory drive becomes a need for self-esteem, or recognition, or achievement. Thus, while exploratory drives may form a foundation for defining motivation, they cannot provide a full explanation.

Motivation as a Learned Behavior

It has been a widely held belief that motivation affects learning, and some attention has been given to the effect of learning on motivation, particularly in trying to understand how

Figure 8. Motivation as learning.

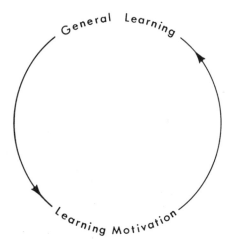

motivation develops. Let me, here, propose a redefinition of motivation: *Motivation equals learning.* Motivation is not only learned, but it is an inseparable part of learning itself. Figure 8 represents this circular relationship.

What I am saying is that people don't learn well if they are not motivated, and they are not motivated because *they never learned how to be motivated.*

There must develop, if motivation levels are to increase, an association process from basic innate drives of hunger, thirst, and the like, to other goals which are as yet unlearned. Thus, the crucial question, What makes a reinforcer reinforcing, or an incentive an incentive? is answered by, It depends on what you learned was motivating. If you never had a learned association between food, praise, self-esteem, and, let's say, money, money would provide no motivation for you.

If you doubt the importance of learned motivation, look at the cross-cultural differences between incentives and behavior. The motivators may be the same general items, but the behaviors that are required to earn them are very different—that is, the learned associations vary. A good example is how need for achievement takes very different directions among other cultures, or even in subcultures within a society. The need is the same, but the learned associations between the need and the corresponding direction of behavior change are different.

This cycle that accounts for these differences has been studied in a slightly different context in terms of how learning is facilitated. It is called "positive transfer," and it is described as the beneficial effect of past learning on new learning. It represents a kind of learning how to learn. This positive transfer is a process that builds from one experience to the next.

What we are suggesting is that not only is there a development of positive transfer for learning as such, but there exists also a positive transfer process for motivation. *The more you learned how to be motivated in the past, the more easily you transfer that motivation* either to new learning, or more importantly, to new levels of incentives. It follows that as your transferring from one level of motivation to another becomes easier, the quality of behavior also changes.

Abandoning Punishment

Before we complete this theoretical section, there are several issues which require further clarification. One of them is the concept and role of punishment.

We have made references on several occasions to the idea of hard and soft management. This is an issue of some intense philosophical controversy in organizations. What kind of leadership gets things done? This is the whole area of applying motivation. Another natural question arises: Where does punishment fit in organizations, and within the concept of motivation?

Anyone who has spent any time in the world knows that punishment techniques are used all the time, and they also know that these techniques work. To deny that punishment affects behavior requires that we overlook the experiences of life. Fear is a real human emotion, and it often results from the anticipation of some form of punishment.

The behaviorists, as we noted earlier, object to punishment on the technical grounds that it conditions for what not to do, and can also have emotional side effects that interfere with the learning process. Their points are well taken, but such a position must be applied with modifications appropriate to both the real world and to common sense.

Ideally, learning, motivation, and human behavior in general are best developed in a positive and supportive environment. Realistically, the world, and in turn our organizations, are not that kind of environment. I personally believe that achieving such a situation is both highly desirable and possible. I try every day to use the positive principles that I preach, but when everything else fails, when I'm at the bottom line, I resort (regress?) to tactics of punishment or threat of punishment.

The fact that this occurs all too frequently must point out the error of attempting to deny the effectiveness of punishment. For every form of positive reinforcement, there is also a negative form that can be used either as punishment or negative reinforcement. It exists as a type of mirror-image:

+	–
praise	criticism
recognition	ignoring
advancement	demotion
paying	fining

One argument against the use of punishment maintained that it doesn't have the lasting quality that reinforcement has. While this is true for some types of behavior, in general, punishment can have lasting effects, and in some cases one or two punishing experiences can exert an influence for an entire lifetime.

Perhaps the most valid reason for minimizing the use of punishment focuses around the idea of satiation. There is some evidence to suggest that the satiation thresholds for punishment are at least as low as for positive reinforcement. That is, the effectiveness of punishment wears out quickly if overused.

The managerial strategist will note that once you have reached a punishment satiation level, you've played your last card. There is nothing else left, and you are rendered powerless to change the situation. Even if you never reach such an extreme, by overusing punishment, just as with positive reinforcement, you reduce its effectiveness.

In taking what I consider to be a realistic position toward punishment, I don't want to imply that positive reinforcement should not be considered as the position of first resort. By all means, it should. Let us not discount the importance of reinforcing what we want people to do, but at the same time, let us realize that there are all sorts of organizational behaviors we don't want people to do as well.

In Defense of Common Sense

To keep from becoming lost in our own jargon, we must continually step back from organizational or individual human relations problems and undertake a common sense analysis. It is too easy to become entrapped in the complexities of human behavior and rendered a victim of too many theories.

Whenever you, as a manager, encounter a human relations problem, remind yourself that there is a reason for behavior and ask yourself these questions: Why is this person acting this way? Are there defenses operating that I'm not seeing, or circumstances that I'm not aware of? Most of all, what is the perception of that person? Answering these questions means tackling the black box problem head on.

Once you have an idea of the reasons for any given behavior, once you have assessed the reinforcements and contingencies that are operating, once you understand the motivation levels and types of needs of the person, you can develop a rational strategy in dealing with the situation.

One group of management scientists has given new importance to a manager's feelings about a problem. It's sometimes referred to as "management by intuition." Its principles center around two factors: taking in the whole picture, and trusting your emotions.

Taking in the whole picture, which we consider in a later chapter, offers the benefit of avoiding a "forest for the trees" problem. As you are able to consider a broader perspective, your own role becomes more clearly defined, and your actions can take on greater long-term applicability. You may, through this perspective, be better able to set motivational priorities for one, two, or even five years for yourself and your people. Even though it has a high probability of being changed as circumstances change, it is this kind of planning that gives a rudder of control to your career and your organization.

We are often reminded that it is the rational mind that is stable and trustworthy, and that our emotions only get in the way of effective functioning. Again, from a common sense perspective, we have both cognitive and affective behaviors, and to deny the affective, or emotional, is to lose a valuable asset as well as to fail to understand an important part of ourselves. True control of our emotions does not result from suppressing them, but from understanding and accepting them in their proper role.

This understanding and acceptance of emotion was supposed to be a function of T-groups as they were originally conceived by industrial psychologists, but the pragmatism and common sense got lost along the way. T-groups were designed to bring managers together in an open and safe setting to discuss their human relations problems, not so much from a rational viewpoint, but from an emotional, or better yet, from a whole person standpoint. This was to give managers a realistic appraisal of their strengths and weaknesses, and in turn make them both more effective and more human.

I think the principles of T-groups from a motivational perspective are still sound. It's how they are conducted and their purpose that need redefining. If their goals are the improvement of self-esteem, increased understanding of yourself as a manager and a person, and new commitments to your job and your life goals, then they have a positive beginning. If they are conducted in a supportive and relatively nonthreatening way, with both group direction and qualified leadership, they may achieve their purpose, namely of improving the intuitive side of management.

Thus, from a common sense point of view, *motivation involves the whole person, and it involves the reasons and circumstances which determine behavior.*

Your Model

After you assess all of these definition problems, it is only natural that you will come away from all this with your own model of motivation and human behavior. Everyone has his own pet theory about people, and some theories are better than others. As I have said or implied a number of times, I don't really have a nice plug-in package for you to take to work with you. Sometimes I wish I did. After all, I could have a new theory and lecture all over the country and make lots of money. The only problem is that what I'd be saying would only be partially true at best. Any neat package must, by its very simplicity, leave something out.

Some of the complexities we are referring to involve the situation. For example, in any analysis of behavior we must ask what are the relevant variables:

The background of the subjects.

The present philosophies and attitudes of the subjects.

The present environment.

The perception of the problem.

The problem.

The conceptual solutions already arrived at.

The ways in which all of these factors interact.

Despite these and other complexities, we all somehow sort them out into patterns and categories. You can do this with varying degrees of background and guidelines. Some managers do this from a gut reaction and their past experiences, others use combinations of formal training and intuitive feelings, and still others shoot from the hip with little or no outside input. No matter what we say here, you will still maintain your own predominant style; that is, you will incorporate our model of motivation into your existing ideas and behaviors, in effect creating a model of our model that fits you.

Due to its individual and subjective nature, I cannot tell you how to incorporate our model or how it will turn out for you. I can, however, offer some guidelines on using your emerging model.

1. Make it portable. Feel comfortable with it. Don't use ideas or techniques that are artificial or contrived relative to your own managerial style. Employees can recognize a cosmetic job a mile away. If, for instance, positive reinforcement such as verbal praise doesn't fit you, don't use it. Use a modification that does feel comfortable, such as a written recommendation.

Whatever techniques you adopt, remember that for them to work you must be able to wear them. There are going to be too many spontaneous decisions and problems that will require an immediate response. You won't be able to look up what you should do in a book. If it isn't part of you, it can't help you when you get in a tight spot because you'll have all you can do to meet the problem head on.

2. Along with the principle of portability comes the concept of internal consistency. One of the stereotypes that we have, rightly or wrongly, about our leaders is that they must be reliable. They must be able to develop some feeling of predictability and order. This kind of reliability is a basic element in the development of trust. If you flutter around from one position to another, or from one principle to another, your people will never feel secure with you. You may think that this

keeps them on their toes, but it may just keep them from committing themselves to your leadership efforts.

3. Whatever your model, learn to test it. A closed model withers on the vine as times and circumstances change. Unless you are sensitive to feedback on the effectiveness of your techniques, you can be rubbing people the wrong way and diminishing your effectiveness, and not even know it. One clause must be added in the interest of pragmatism: Use your head, and test your modifications in relative safety. Make use of trial balloons. Don't go out on a limb needlessly because it will only make you gun-shy if the branch breaks, and that, in turn, will increase the probability of opting for a closed system.

4. After you test new ideas for your model, evaluate them with checks and balances. We all want to regard ourselves as the best judges of our own behavior, but unfortunately we often are not. In addition to your own evaluation, test results can come from employees, colleagues, and outside confidants. If your pride gets in the way, you may see your seeking input and advice as a weakness, but you can seek counsel, often indirectly, without compromising your position with another person. I've seen this done, and have done it myself, in such a way that the person giving the advice isn't even aware of it. He is really receiving only as much information as I choose to offer, and in the process I'm picking his brains about my own behavior.

To keep your model broad-based, you should have a plan for three basic evaluations of behavior:

Positive. The behavior you have assessed is superior to what you expected, and you want to encourage that sort of performance in the future.

Neutral. The behavior is satisfactory and progressing well, and you want to keep it that way.

Negative. The behavior is below your expectations and standards, and you want to see it improve.

From any one of these three perspectives, you have evaluated where you are, and now you want to define the motivational plan that will get you where you want to go. What you need is either of these three programs:

DAP—developmental action program. This is designed to expand motivation from a positive performance base.

MAP—maintenance action program. This approach encourages continuance and stability.

RAP—remedial action program. This is designed to correct and increase performance that has been assessed negatively.

Any of the principles we have presented will fit for either a DAP, MAP, or RAP strategy, but how you implement the principles depends on your assessment of the behavior, and your assessment is directly related to the definitions in your personal model.

You can see from this brief discussion that what goes into your model is often subtle and complex. If you are ever to understand the cause and effect relationship between your actions and your results as a manager, you need to be aware of the dynamics of your model and its influence on your management.

part two
Practice

6
Behavioral
Engineering

MOST good managers that I've known are also good teachers. Performance appraisal, delegation, communication, human relations, and motivation all involve the elements of teaching, guiding, and planning. Of course, it is not enough for a good teacher to teach "how." Teaching "why" is just as crucial. As one psychologist has said, we don't teach a rat *how* to press a bar; it already knows that. We teach it to *want* to press a bar. Well, a manager doesn't first teach a person how to load cartons, or write, or develop judgment; he must tell the employee why and then, if necessary, how.

Motivation, then, does not involve the "how" of behavior; rather, it involves the "why" that is right for the individual. Even with the "why," an employee may not become competent. However, competence is better obtained with motivation present than without it, since part of being competent involves behavior, and of course that means there is a role for motivation.

Figure 9. Elements of behavioral engineering.

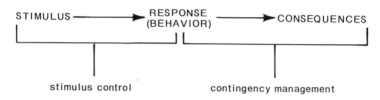

Stimulus Control and Contingency Management

In the broader context of the manager as a teacher, the identification of the learning environment becomes important. This is where the idea of *behavioral engineering* comes in. Behavioral engineering (BE) is simply the application of the principles of behavior to pragmatic problems. As shown in Figure 9, there are two technologies involved in BE, *stimulus control and contingency management.*

What does this diagram represent? For one thing, it shows the interrelationship of stimulus control and reinforcement (contingencies). It can be translated into three simple rules of behavioral engineering:

1. The employee must make the response that is to be learned (behavior).
2. The responses must be strengthened (reinforced).
3. The stimuli that occasion the response must be identified (stimulus control).

How can a manager translate these ideas into actual practice? One approach, a variation of management by objectives, involves using what are called *behavioral objectives.* It is a type of behavioral engineering that can increase your performance appraisal effectiveness, help you and your employer to plan and organize, and take you the first step toward becoming a manager of behavior.

What are behavioral objectives? *They are specific overt*

behaviors which serve to identify the direction and satisfactory accomplishment of a goal. In setting behavioral objectives, the manager must ask:

1. What are the responses to be learned? The best approach is to require as much overt activity as possible. This allows the manager to reinforce *behavior* and not *inferences* about potential behavior.

2. What will be the criterion for reinforcement? The manager must know what behavior should get reinforced. This prevents administering reinforcement inappropriately, or strengthening und.sired behavior.

3. What stimuli are supposed to precede the response? The circumstances under which the behavior is to occur are very important. The right behavior at the wrong time is not effective behavior management.

Once these three questions have been addressed, the manager is ready to set up specific guidelines for writing behavioral objectives. This step may be for the manager's own use, or it may be for subsequent performance appraisal of the employee. In the latter case the manager must develop the behavioral objectives in concert with the employee. This is the only fair way that management can hold employees responsible for delegated objectives.

Keep in mind that the guidelines that follow are simply a way of organizing your behavior and the behavior of other people in accordance with the principles of learning. There isn't much point in trying to manage behavior by working against these principles. If your job as a manager is frustrating, unpleasant, and stressful, it probably has some strong currents either from you, your employees, or your boss, that are causing you to swim upstream constantly.

After answering the three previous questions about behavioral objectives, the manager should be able to translate the data into the following guidelines for well-stated behavioral objectives:

Behavior. This is the specific overt performance. This performance must be stated in such a way that it can be observed and measured. Examples of terms indicating behavior are "list," "finish," "design," "direct."

Condition. These specify the environment within which the behaviors are to occur. For example: "*From* the available material . . . ," "*Using* the new job description . . . ," "*Given* the engineering specifications. . . ."

Standard. The standard states how well the behavior must be performed in order for the contingencies to apply. It states what level of attainment is required. Examples of standards include "within .01 tolerances," "a maximum of 10 percent scrap," "between levels 6 and 10," "by July 15."

Each of these three elements can now be combined to form a complete behavioral objective such as "List the salary ranges using the new job descriptions between levels 6 and 10" or "Design these housings given the engineering specifications within .01 tolerances."

It should be clear how these behavioral objectives fit into the diagram of behavioral engineering. Too often we require performance and give incomplete or ambiguous directives such as "Improve your attitude" or "Finish the subassemblies" or "Work at this until I give you something else." In each of these cases there is either a behavior, condition, or standard missing; that is, there is a lack of stimulus control or of contingency management. That is poor behavioral engineering.

If, as a manager, you don't understand and control your working environment through some type of behavioral engineering, then don't blame anyone else when the situation gets out of control. It is fair to say that one part of leadership responsibility is to make things happen, not to watch things happen. No matter what your level of authority, within your own realm you are responsible for that piece of the world, be it an entire company, a department, a family, or just yourself.

One interesting paradox about the management of behavior often arises in round-table discussions of these principles, when someone asks, "Aren't these methods awfully autocratic?" Well, this is an involved question. Certainly the *techniques* of managing have an effect on the *style* of management as well as the reverse being true, but the style and the techniques are not one and the same. Just as with any tool, behavior management technology depends on how you use it. If you have a democratic style of supervision, you will involve your employees in setting behavioral objectives and in evaluating the appropriateness of certain contingencies. If you're a tough autocrat, your behavioral engineering approach will reflect this. The paradoxical element here is that, in general, the better their behavioral engineering, the more effective managers become, and the less they rely on manipulative and coercive styles of supervision. So good behavior management can result in *less* and not more overt control.

Developing the Right Behavioral Objectives

The effect that behavioral objectives have on your behavioral engineering efforts as a manager will directly depend on how realistic those objectives are. BE efforts must include an analysis of the current "stimulus yields behavior yields consequence" variables in any given situation. Your analysis must be able to answer the question, Where are we right now? in terms of this three-part sequence. This is often referred to as "establishing your baseline conditions," and it follows the old planning cliché of first knowing where you are before you decide where you want to go.

Knowledge of your baseline conditions will give you a measure of the distance between where you are and where your boss-imposed or system-imposed goals expect you to be at some time in the future. Once this "gap" has been established, your planning efforts can begin. You will be able to develop a *shaping* strategy by planning the steps or successive approximations toward the goal.

The core of your BE planning must center around diagnosing reinforcers. One approach is to first develop a reinforcement menu for each level in Maslow's hierarchy of needs. Here is a list of sample reinforcers that could match the need levels of your people:

Physical reinforcers. Money, movie pass, free coffee, lunch passes.

Safety and security reinforcers. Fringe benefits, seniority lists, specialization, opportunities.

Belongingness and love reinforcers. Invitations to coffee or lunch, recognition in house organ.

Self-esteem reinforcers. Informal and formal recognition, private office, solicitations of advice.

Self-actualization reinforcers. Work on personal projects, job with more achievement possibilities, special assignments.

As you can see from this list, many of the items are reinforcers that you have either thought of using or actually used in the past, but most managers don't scale these to the need levels and concerns of their people. In Chapter 2 I said that dividing this hierarchy into two sections could help to locate the needs of employees more effectively. While this is true generally, a further refinement is necessary for our purposes here.

To one degree or another, people are concerned with all of Maslow's needs. Thus, it then becomes a matter of evaluating an individual's *primary* position on the hierarchy, while at the same time realizing that there may also be need levels of *secondary* concern. For example, suppose a person were trying to satisfy the primary needs for safety and security. The primary needs below them, the physiological level, might already be satisfied. Therefore, any remaining needs would be secondary. Satisfaction, then, depends on using reinforcers in three ways:

1. Maintain reinforcers at the levels below primary concern.
2. Build and strengthen reinforcers at the primary level.

3. Develop shaping reinforcers at the levels above primary concern.

In other words, if you evaluated an employee's primary level at safety and security, you would maintain the physiological need reinforcers, concentrate on the safety and security reinforcers, and introduce successively belongingness and love, self-esteem, and self-actualization reinforcers. This may sound like an awfully complicated and unwieldy procedure, but it is simply a step-by-step walk-through of what managers who are good shapers of behavior do all the time. You may have engaged in this very same process without being conscious of the dynamics behind the effect that you produced.

Once you have made an estimate of the reinforcers that may work for an employee, you are ready to sit down and develop behavioral objectives with that person. Keep in mind that there is a sequence here. A behavioral engineering analysis should lead to some form of behavioral objective that will provide the employee with reinforcement if it is achieved. Too many attempts at setting objectives fail because they have not been preceded by an adequate BE analysis.

Of course, a final test of your BE analysis and behavioral objectives will be the actions that occur. This, after all, is the actual behavior that is the point of all this planning. As Peter Drucker has said, all plans must "degenerate into work." Without the actual behavior, you have no accountability, measurement of results, or feedback. You have no job performance. Once you do have some type of behavior, however, you have the type of feedback that will allow you to evaluate the effectiveness of your BE efforts.

The Premack Principle

The type of shaping that we have implied when referring to primary and secondary needs involves what could be called a "transformation analysis." The shaping has a purpose. Its end goal is actually the achievement of functional autonomy. You will recall that functional autonomy was the transformation of motives from external reinforcement to internal reinforcement. Analyzing the conditions that need to be shaped in order for a person to reach a stage of functional autonomy is what a transformation analysis is all about.

The first step in this analysis is to evaluate the separate reinforcers that relate to the current behavior. There is often more than one, and they may be bunched together. This bunching, or "chaining," can occur naturally or it can be introduced artificially by the manager. Building one reinforcer onto or from another is called the *Premack principle,* for the psychologist who identified the procedure.

The Premack principle specifically involves dividing high probability behavior and low probability behavior into two categories. From a performance standpoint the manager wants the employee to engage in both behaviors. For instance, an employee must sort the incoming mail, a dull routine job, and must also prepare a variance report to be submitted to the vice president of personnel, an interesting job with high recognition value. The first task would be classified as "low probability behavior," and the second as "high probability." The Premack method would advise that the high probability behavior be contingent upon the low probability behavior. In this way, the second task becomes a reinforcer for the first. This is how reinforcers chain to one another and build from simple reinforcements into functionally autonomous behavior.

This chaining, Premack style, has been around a long while; it is simply a matter of developing a system. Parents often use this approach when they set up a chain of behavior prerequisites such as, "You can go out and play only after you've finished your supper." This is pairing a weak behavior with a strong behavior, thereby adding strength to the former.

Using the Premack system can give you good performance on routine work if there are also interesting parts to the job as a whole that can be paired with the less exciting tasks. With this approach a little job enrichment could go a long way because the enriched work is high probability behavior, and the low probability behavior attached to it would improve as a result.

Effective Feedback

A second step in a transformation analysis involves feedback and reinforcement. In most cases, feedback serves as a reinforcement, or as a punishment for behavior that has just occurred, but the type and style of the feedback can determine the *progress* of the behavior as well as the maintenance of it. The point is that feedback must be designed for the shaping purposes you have in mind. Questions such as, What type of feedback? When is the feedback given? and How is it given? are important in the shaping process.

Answers to the feedback question deal with styles and approaches that border on being in the category of an art. After all, the finer points of feedback technique can be viewed as the major vehicle for staff development, and good leaders recognize the need for progressive development of their people. Personal influence centers around the value another individual places on your feedback—your reactions pro or con.

Informal feedback is usually verbal, and its impact is increased if it is also social. That is, if the feedback is given to an employee in the presence of others, the effect, for good or for ill, is stronger. Praise means more and criticism seems harsher when they occur in the context of a group. The reason centers around an additional factor that is present in a group that isn't as directly relevant in a one-to-one encounter: *social evaluation apprehension,* the fear of being evaluated negatively by others. The sensitive manager knows how this apprehension operates, and how to use it.

Formal feedback is usually written and takes the form of memos, correspondence, and performance review. While formal feedback systems may have more of a designated purpose than informal feedback, in both cases the shaping impact is not often considered in advance. Most performance review sessions have no reliable assessment of the effects this type of feedback will have on future behavior. Rather they evaluate past behavior and assume that the review technique will incorporate future actions all under the same umbrella. This rarely works out, since it is not designed as a shaping tool toward progressive staff development even if the review procedure is conducted by the manager with a positive attitude. The formal system must change as the behavior changes or else it will only serve a *historical* role and not a *functional* role.

Many managers pass up a powerful opportunity to shape behavior through the formal performance appraisal system. They often resent the obligation to evaluate their people, and become preoccupied with filling in the little boxes with check marks for "needs improvement," "satisfactory," "above average," and "excellent." That is, they become hung up on the *form* of the system rather than the *process* of performance review.

Specifically, the manager can use what we know about behavioral engineering to get more mileage out of performance appraisal. Firstly, we know that *delay of reinforcement is the major enemy of any shaping effort.* Thus, semiannual or even quarterly performance review is fine for personnel records and documentation, but it is too long an interval to effectively shape daily or weekly behavior. The longer the interval between the behavior and the consequences, the weaker the association and, in turn, the less effective the learning.

Decreasing the delay of reinforcement may only involve a more continuous and frequent feedback procedure. This can work very well if behavioral objectives are used by the employee to measure weekly performance. We are not suggesting here that a manager adopt a close style of supervision. *Good short-term behavioral objectives provide their own supervision.* All the manager needs is a reporting system for two-way communication of the objective's results.

Whatever system the individual manager develops, the important point is that a periodic quarterly or semiannual performance appraisal will include two sets of information as input: (1) the manager's broad overall evaluation of the employee and (2) the cumulative subsets of weekly results. This way there are no dramatic surprises, and the manager can shape the bulk of the behavior soon after it occurs rather than after the period of time has elapsed. It is not realistic to expect a single periodic appraisal to deal with what we might call the increments of behavior. That is, using the Premack system and the progressive transformation of motives approach requires much more day-to-day development than the periodic appraisal system can offer. No wonder an annual performance review fails then when we expect it to do something it's not designed or able to do.

A Little Lecture on Your Role

After hearing about some of these behavioral engineering principles, many managers react by saying:

> That's a nice system, but if I could devote that much time and effort to my people I wouldn't have a problem in the first place. I just can't afford the time, and even if I could, it really wouldn't be good for me to establish the dependency relationship that is required for these ideas to work.

I would answer this kind of a response in several ways. Firstly, of course, time, effort, and commitment are involved. What do you think staff development is, anyway, if it's not a dedication to your people? Often your own reinforcement for such commitment will only come from self-satisfaction and not from external appreciation. Not every employee will recognize or even respond to your efforts, and if you require that kind of support in order to justify the time and effort, maybe *you* don't have enough functional autonomy as a leader.

The second consideration reflected in the statement "I just can't afford the time" is that as a manager you are probably already devoting as much time as a behavioral engineering effort could take, except that you're not getting the results you could if you had such a system. You may be surprised to find out how much of your time is devoted to monitoring, correcting, planning, and reorganizing employee behavior. In fact, you might find you have enough time to construct a behavioral engineering plan if you compared the effort it would take to the time you already spend with employees. It may even be that you can't afford the time precisely *because* you don't have a BE system. It may just be that your boss feels the organization can't promote someone who is unable to develop employees, in which case your not being able to afford the time and effort may turn out to be a rather costly saving to you in the long run.

Lastly, the point about establishing a dependency relationship is simply a misconception about behavioral engineering. Its purpose is the transformation of motives that we have called "functional autonomy." Dependency and autonomy are incompatible. If behavioral engineering doesn't shape toward progressive internal motivation, it will eventually lose its effectiveness. Why? Because of satiation. A static or nonprogressive reinforcement strategy will soon wear out. This is when managers resort to horizontal movement—more on the same level—because the same amount of the same type of reinforcement doesn't work forever. When horizontal movement becomes an exclusive tool, *then* dependency is a problem.

Furthermore, if a transformation is taking place, by definition internal motivation is less dependent on outside or external support. You see, external and internal motivations do not often exist simultaneously for the same behavior. While there may be an interaction of the two, the effect is not cumulative. In fact, they may even cancel each other out.

Finally, on this point, when managers tell me about a concern for not establishing a dependency relationship, it often means that there has been a problem of this kind in the past, perhaps brought on by the managers' own style. This point may be clarified as follows: If a manager fosters or demands dependency to begin with, his possible abuse of BE tools can exaggerate this dependency. Such an effect, however, is not inherent in BE. It is safe to generalize that a manager with such a predisposition would do this with almost any behavioral strategy. However, the fact that the bad manager may become worse through using more effective methods of control is not really a justification for not improving the skills of a manager.

I may be leaving the impression of being a bit impatient, and even harsh, with managers who resist the use of BE. In a way, I am. This resistance, I feel, is caused not by any inability to "see" the principles behind BE, but by their overall managerial attitude. The attitude is just this: "If it isn't easy for me to learn and use, I don't want to know about it." Too many managers represent the proverbial river taking the path of least resistance. Effective management cannot be guided by such an attitude.

The implication here is not that every good manager must have a martyr complex, but neither does good self or staff development occur automatically or spontaneously. It is guided. Spontaneous development does happen, but it may or may not be beneficial to the organization or the individual. There are too many interfering variables in unplanned development to make it a sound strategy. Since this development must be deliberate, and often it does not receive external support, there is a certain commitment that is a prerequisite. Fewer and fewer managers are willing to make and sustain the necessary effort.

One more consideration at the risk of excessive moralizing, since the point has been made and we will not beat it to death. It's simply that this effort and commitment is at the core of the definition of management. So many traditional definitions talk about getting things done through people, or organizing resources, but they miss the most important part in any of these approaches: *Good management is serving your people.* The word "serving" is used deliberately to connote the role of effort and commitment. Without the idea of service, we have organizations with individual managers operating in a power-oriented, independent, and random fashion. If you believe that organizations are effective because they form a Gestalt—a whole which is more than just the sum of its parts—then you should

recognize that managerial isolation in terms of people development is at odds with that type of philosophy.

As has been suggested previously, maybe it is a question of
functional autonomy of the manager. Perhaps the *motivation
to serve* is not properly developed by senior management. We
have all heard over and over that lack of development from the
top affects the hourly employee eventually. Thus, as with many
strategies, BE must be an organization-wide effort if significant
changes are to be realized.

And yet, the senior managerial motivation problem cannot
be used by the manager as an escape from, or an excuse to
avoid being concerned about, staff development. As a fellow
management consultant, Paul Illman, has said, "There may be
chaos above me, but that doesn't mean there has to be chaos
below me."

7
Real Life Limitations

AFTER having patiently proceeded to this point, you may be asking yourself, "How do these principles translate into effective practice in organizational settings?" The translation process has a number of facets, and in any specific situation one or more of the principles we've discussed may present certain limitations. Yet even with the limitations, dramatic results can be obtained. In fact, the limitations may be the key to the successful use of those principles.

Emery Air Freight

The Emery Air Freight experience[1] provides an example of the successful use of feedback procedures based on the principles

[1]"At Emery Air Freight: Positive Reinforcement Boosts Performance," *Organizational Dynamics,* winter 1973, pp. 41-50.

outlined at the end of Chapter 5. Edward Feeney, who was vice president of the company at the time, was the primary force behind the new program of feedback and positive reinforcement, which is reported to have saved Emery $2 million in three years.

As an air freight forwarder, Emery is heavily involved in container shipping. Given the cost factors of air freight, effective utilization of these containers is essential. Feeney discovered that despite all the efforts of industrial engineering at Emery, most of the warehouse people were not using empty container space to best advantage.

All employees had been through an extensive training program with emphasis on this function, and yet their perception of how well they used container space was very different from the actual situation. Most of the managers and workers estimated their usage rate for the containers at about 90 percent. When Feeney and his team studied usage, they put the figure at closer to 45 percent. One of their first efforts was to provide the employees with a self-feedback checklist. The checklist identified *behaviorally* the key performance-related items that were labeled as problem areas. As a result of this *one* action, in the first year, container utilization increased to the point of saving an estimated $500,000.

The second step at Emery was to train managers to use the techniques of positive reinforcement that were discussed in Chapter 3. Emery prepared an in-house course dealing with recognition and rewards which used, among other things, a reinforcement menu of 150 items from a smile of encouragement, to buying coffee, to involved praise for good performance.

Under this system of accurate feedback and positive reinforcement, which was *contingent* upon performance, improvement was reflected in visible cost savings of considerable significance. Feeney is now a private consultant in this field, advising other organizations how this approach can be adapted to their situations.

The Emery experience focused on only two aspects of the principles we examined in Part I and will apply more in the chapters that follow, but first, further refinement of the limits of those basic ideas is necessary to avoid that fragmented cookbook approach that makes motivation a myth rather than a successful reality.

The Ability Problem

Adapting principles to the right situation, to the right people, and at the right time is the art of motivation. This means knowing what motivation techniques to use, whom to use them on, and when to use them. This all reduces down to identifications of people and situations and to understanding the parameters and limitations of the tools available to a manager. Let us address some of those limitations.

The first limitation of the manager is related to *motivating for ability or competence*. This is not impossible, but on the other hand, it's not entirely possible either. In Chapter 5 the point was made that it is more important to teach "why." Although this is almost always true in lower level jobs, it does not hold as the skill requirements increase. Performance then depends on ability and motivation, as expressed in this formula:

$$\text{performance} = \text{ability} + \text{motivation}$$

What this means is that there is an *interaction* between two individual factors, ability and motivation, which is responsible for performance. That interaction becomes more important as ability requirements increase. The well-known industrial psychologist Edward Lawler explains:

> . . . not all performance problems that occur in organizations are caused by low motivation. Often, particularly in higher-level jobs, with performance problems of individuals in organizations, it is crucial to try to find out how much of the problem is due to poor ability. . . . If aptitude is low, then there is no way to improve performance.[2]

[2]*Motivations in Work Organizations*, Monterey, Calif., Brooks/Cole Publishing, 1973, p. 9.

Lawler maintains that

$$ability = (training + experience) \times aptitude$$

Therefore, since ability interacts with motivation, then training, experience, and aptitude also interact with motivation in much the same way.

What all this is saying, then, is that, at least to some degree, the influence of motivation is limited; it can't solve all your problems. Motivation is a facilitator, so it needs something to facilitate, namely, ability. Our point here follows the old saying that you just can't make chicken salad out of chicken fat. You need something to start with. I'm sorry, but you can't make a custodian a company president through motivation alone.

Personally, on this problem of interaction I happen to feel that motivation and ability are not equally weighted. My own prejudices, of course, lead me to value the impact of motivation more highly than the other factors since it serves as more of an umbrella for at least the training and experience aspects of ability. In other words, motivation influences, through facilitation or debilitation, the effect of training and experience.

The aspect of aptitude presents more of a problem. This is the area where motivation will have the least effect, provided that we define "aptitude" in a strict constructionist sense as *natural potential*. By this definition, aptitude is a built-in (genetic perhaps) fixed trait and therefore is not subject to the influence of motivation. For example, no amount of motivation will make a mentally retarded person a gifted scholar. (A retarded person who improves does so through training and experience, not through increasing aptitude.) Again, I must interject a personal comment on this issue. As psychologists, we are not at all sure what role aptitude really has in affecting behavior since we can't measure it well. This situation is well illustrated by the current I.Q. controversies which question the reliability of the entire concept.

For the manager, the aptitude question is only important in higher level job classifications, and even then its role is not at all clear. The other two parts of ability, training and experience, are more relevant in organizational staff development. The most enthusiastic employees may fail needlessly if the manager has not properly assessed their training and experience relative to the requirements of the job. It isn't fair to expect motivation to fill in this gap.

The Selection Process

After the ability-motivation limitation is considered, this question must be asked: To what degree is the manager responsible for and capable of changing the motivation of employees? In the context of this book the answer is, There is a great responsibility, and a great capability given certain guidelines. However, within these guidelines there are limitations. As Peter Drucker points out: "No business enterprise is competent, let alone obligated, to substitute its efforts for the self-development efforts of the individual. To do this would not only be unwarranted paternalism; it would be foolish pretension."[3]

The idea that the whole responsibility for motivation does not rest with the manager or even the organization makes sense if we consider the wide variety of factors that influence motivation. In general, developmental experiences, role models, cultural conditioning, family characteristics, and individual differences all play their part. An employee doesn't come into an organization as a tabula rasa, a blank slate. It is for this reason that one overriding consideration is added.

The *selection of people* must have the limits of motivation as its foundation. Consider, for example, an employee you would initially describe as an External, low n Achiever, who could work well under Theory X assumptions. To select that employee for a job that requires an Internal, high n Achiever, who needs Theory Y assumptions, is to overestimate the organization's

[3]*Management: Tasks, Responsibilities, Practices,* New York, Harper & Row, 1974, p. 427.

ability to effect a transition of motives—that is, to develop functional autonomy—in an employee.

Again Lawler expands on this point:

> Probably the best opportunity organizations have to influence the needs of their employees is provided by the selection process. It suggests that rather than trying to change the needs of their subordinates, managers should concentrate on placing people in jobs where their need structure is appropriate.[4]

Often, the manager tries to do too much by way of trying to alter patterns of motivation that the employee has. There is an approach used by many successful managers that is designed to get the most mileage out of the strengths that are already present in the person or the organization. That approach is known as "organic development."

Organic Development

The abbreviation OD is traditionally used to mean "organizational development." A major premise behind OD techniques is that through active leadership of the structure and the dynamics of an organization, performance will be enhanced. My reaction to such a premise is 100 percent positive. Yet, at the same time, there is a complementary counterpart to active OD, and that is passive OD, or *organic development*.

The word "organic" is important. As used here it relates to organisms. A living organism is viable, or capable of biological growth. *At their best, organizations, like organisms, are capable of growth.* Perhaps much of that growth occurs without active organizational control and could be used to better advantage than is now the case. A couple of examples of actual situations will illustrate this concept of organic development better than a conceptual explanation.

[4]*Motivations in Work Organizations*, p. 38.

Case 1

The first case was reported some time ago by a psychologist named Donald Roy, who took a job as an operator of a clicking machine in a manufacturing plant to study organizational behavior. He worked closely with three other men: Sammy, Ike, and George. In the following excerpt from his report, the word "times" refers to predictable but unscheduled breaks.

> My attention was first drawn to this "times" business . . . when I was encouraged to join in the sharing of two peaches. Sammy provided the peaches from his lunch box after making the announcement, "Peach time!" . . . Sammy continued to provide the peaches and . . . Ike invariably complained about the quality of the fruit, and his complaints fed the fires of continued banter. . . . I felt, before I achieved insight into the function of peach time, that Ike was showing poor manners by looking a gift horse in the mouth.

> Banana time followed peach time by approximately an hour. Sammy again provided the refreshments. . . . There was, however, no four-way sharing of Sammy's banana. Ike would gulp it down by himself after extracting it from Sammy's lunch box. . . . Each morning, after making the snatch, Ike would call out, "Banana time" and proceed to down his prize.[5]

Roy also describes other "times," such as window time, where Ike would open the window next to Sammy to let in the fresh air and Sammy would complain about the cold. George would enter into the dispute, usually supporting Ike. Of course, Sammy would complain about the window whether it was winter or summer, and he always brought his peaches and banana.

The purpose of these "times" was demonstrated when they were temporarily discontinued because Ike and Sammy had

[5]Banana Time: Job Satisfaction and Informal Interaction," *Human Organization,* vol. 18, no. 4, pp. 156-168.

an actual argument and weren't on speaking terms. Roy describes the boredom and fatigue of the long and unsatisfying week of work without the breaks. This changed immediately after Sammy and Ike made up and reinstituted the "times."

Now no manager had anything whatever to do with this natural organic development. In fact, managerial presence would have been an interference. Furthermore, no manager could have deliberately contrived this kind of interaction. It was a spontaneous relationship with a purpose. Roy found that productivity, on his part anyway, fell during that week of silence.

The sensitive manager will be aware of the human interactions, such as the banter between Sammy and Ike, that occur in an organization. It is relatively easy to suppress this kind of behavior on the rationale that it is inefficient and counterproductive, and some of it is. The process of differentiating productive organic development from nonproductive is an important motivational technique. Many managers today would agree that organic interactions like those of Sammy and Ike serve a purpose and may be left intact, but not all situations are as clear-cut, as our second case will demonstrate.

Case 2

Let's say that at one work station of an automobile assembly line there were four people assigned, and their job was putting on lens covers for the side signal lights. As each car came down the line to this station, each person put on one cover. The rate of cars on an assembly line is steady, and as a result, breaks could be taken only when a worker was relieved by a utility person, someone who has the job of substituting. Sometimes a utility would be available immediately, and sometimes it would take 30 minutes before the utility could be pulled off another relief job. (Each area had a limited number of utilities.)

Organically, without management sanction or direction, the people on the lens operation came up with a technique, known as "doubling up," to resolve the utility problem. Two people instead of four worked on the line putting on not one but two lens covers. Because this meant actually doubling up the work load, they had to be relieved in a short time so they decided on one-hour work shifts. After the hour, the other two would work the double load, and so the alternating went throughout the day.

During their hour off, the two people could talk or just generally relax. One could go to the bathroom or for coffee, but at least one of the two remained at the work station even though they were on break. Morale was high.

This practice was eventually forbidden by both management and the labor union even though quality control reported a significant improvement in the lens cover operation. The workers themselves had two explanations for the quality improvement. Firstly, since working on a double schedule was so demanding, they didn't have time to be distracted or daydream as they did at half the pace before doubling up. That is, they paid more attention to their work. Secondly, if they did miss a cover, they simply signaled to the person on break to catch it before the next station. That person would correct the error and add that to time worked, thus earning more break time.

As you may have already guessed, management was against doubling up because it meant that these people were actually working only four hours a day. No self-respecting high need for achievement manager can accept such a situation. Management simply had a gut reaction against paying someone for eight hours who had only worked four. The implications scared it. This was an organic development that it couldn't accept, and no amount of reasoning in terms of paying for performance and not time could change its mind.

The labor union was opposed to the practice for fear of management exploitation—that is, it was afraid management would say, "OK, if you can work that hard for four hours, then you should be able to do it for six or eight." Thus, union paternalism intervened to protect the interests of the worker even if the worker didn't realize them.

Who was right in this situation is hard to say, but the effects were clear. After doubling up was banned, certain feelings became evident among the workers. They felt:

1. More like *Externals* who were subject to the control of others.
2. *Punished* for trying to do a better job.
3. That management had no intentions of *rewarding* the human element of work.

From this standpoint, it is safe to say that it may not have been what management did that was crucial, but rather how they did it in terms of the *perspective of the employees.*

Further impact of the ban on doubling up was to be felt a few months later when the entire auto plant went out on strike, with this issue as a major catalyst. Currently, the workers still double up, but they do so "under cover." They go through the motions of working to pacify the management and union leadership, but only half of them are really working at one time.

Handling Organic Development

I think Case 2 demonstrates the mess that can be generated when managers are insensitive to the organic element of the working environment. There will always be some situations developing that may not serve the organization's interests, but it is equally true that there is a reason why they develop in the first place. That is, organic developments are often symptoms of something else. A good manager will scrape the surface to understand the underlying purpose that the behavior serves. Keep in mind that I am not talking about psychiatry here; nor am I suggesting the manager undertake an effort to understand the causes of all human behavior. Rather, I am calling for an analysis rather than a superficial observation.

In both Cases 1 and 2, the reasons behind the behavior were closely tied to the nature of the job, and the particular type of behavior was tied to the nature of the individuals involved. Both jobs were routine and boring, requiring an infinitesimal amount of cerebral activity. In both, there was almost no feeling of control over rewards and punishments, yet with the organic development the job became bearable. In each case the method was individualized. The banter of Sammy and Ike may not have worked at all on the auto assembly line; nor would the doubling up have been effective for the clicking machine operations.

What does this individuation mean? It means that organic development *must stay* organic or else it becomes contrived and ineffective. This is a powerful limitation of the manager, and the best way to deal with it is to leave as much of it alone as you can afford to. It also means that because this behavior is spontaneously organic, there are no neat formulas for training a manager to use it properly.

There is, however, one good general guideline to follow in an effort to be sensitive to organic processes. It is the old rule that if you really want to understand a problem on the firing line or in the field, *ask the people who are there.* They know much more about all the little details and implications of their jobs than you, and if they are not punished for offering you organic insights into their situations, they will soon open up with the kind of locked-away information that other managers never have access to because they're not aware of the richness of this treasure. These people can give you insights that will make you seem like the slickest troubleshooter in the organization.

Sometimes the smallest of small talk or the seemingly most insignificant observations of the rank and file worker turn out to be useful information in getting a feel for what's happening. Personally, I know that if I want to get a handle on the workings of a company, the first people I talk to are the secretaries. They know everything that's going on, and they will tell you if their instincts tell them it's safe to do so. That's, of course, where style and approach would come in, but let's get back to the symptoms that organic development can represent.

You should treat the symptoms of negative organic development by looking at the job, the people, and the situation, not by developing strategies to counter organic problems. Systems like behavioral engineering don't work well on organic development, but they do work on problems of reinforcement, punishment, job content, autonomy, and objectives—problems that cause negative organic development. These are your proper concern, so don't waste a lot of time and effort trying to use techniques of motivation and behavior management on the symptoms, which negative organic development represents. If you do, you'll be making your own contribution to the myths of motivation.

The Job and the Person

As I maintained earlier in this chapter, the manager does not bear the entire responsibility for motivating employees. After analyzing the employee's behavior, implementing behavioral objectives, and shaping with rewards and punishments, and after developing rewards to increase functional autonomy, the manager must say, "OK, now show me!" The employee is thus put into a results-contingent situation; that is, he must face a sink-or-swim test based on results. Of course, this is also a test of the manager's efforts, but the employee may fail even if the manager has done everything right. Some people just don't make it. Even an optimistic humanist like Maslow came to that conclusion:

> Maslow learned from his experience with graduate students at Brandeis that freedom could be growth-producing for some, but for others seemed to produce negative results. It was what he called the "continental-divide principle"—it either made them or broke them. For the already healthy individual, stress and challenge were growth producing; but for the insecure, weak individual this was not the answer. Apparently, people can be benefited by challenge only if the challenge does not exceed their personal limits.[6]

[6]Frank Goble, *The Third Force*, New York, Pocket Books, 1971, p. 63.

In organizations, those personal limits Maslow was referring to involve an interaction between the job and the person in which the two either enhance or limit one another. If the person cannot fulfill the challenge of the job, the job suffers. At the same time, personal growth does not receive the proper nutrients and it too suffers. The same doubly negative effects occur if, conversely, the job limits the person. Obviously, the manager must work within the context of these two factors.

Just as the person has a development hierarchy (such as Maslow's, given the modifications suggested previously), so also does the job itself. Rather than "a hierarchy," it would be better labeled "a cycle." The first stage in this cycle is the *honeymoon phase.* This is equivalent to an orientation period where the new employee is not expected to actually do very much except become familiar with the organization and the new job. Depending on the job level, this may last from one day to several weeks. Usually the more complex the job, the longer the phase.

After orientation, a probationary period usually follows— the *make-or-break phase.* This is the time in which judgments are made as to whether or not the person can really cut it. The job and person may not be matched right, requiring a transfer, demotion, or firing.

Assuming the person survives the probationary period, the next stage is often the *on-top-of-the-job phase.* Now the employee is well-grounded and tested. There develops an understanding of how to get things done, and new ideas start to take shape. A kind of harmony develops between the person and the organization. Ideally, this phase should last forever, but it often does not.

Once the person leaves the on-top-of-the-job phase, a *leveling-off phase* develops. Here the employee is still performing adequately, but the hum has gone out of the wheels. The new ideas don't come so regularly, and a pattern of easing off becomes visible.

The last stage that appears is the *in-a-rut phase.* After leveling off, the employee is just providing minimal performance, usually enough work to avoid dismissal. But this type of person is the deadwood that gets cut first in any reorganizing efforts.

It is by no means inevitable that an employee go through this cycle completely or exactly as described. The complete cycle does, however, occur frequently among both line and staff people, at a rate depending on the person and the job.

Motivationally, if your people are not in the on-top-of-the-job phase, you have three choices: (1) Accept the situation and get what performance you can, (2) enrich or revitalize the job in an effort to start the cycle from the beginning again, or (3) get rid of the person.

A fourth option that is often attempted, and equally as often fails, is to "motivate" the person, that is, to try to rearrange the person's hierarchical need levels somehow. This may seem like a possibility, given the principle that shaping can occur in either direction on a hierarchy, but the effort and risk aren't worth it when it's really the job, not the person, that needs changing. It's the old "mountain to Mohammed" problem. Why change the person to fit the job, when what the cycle indicates is the need to fit the job to the person?

The most important limitation here is that as a manager, you often don't have the power to completely change a job for one of your employees. In that case you must compromise by behaviorally engineering the job as close as possible to the level of motivation of your employee, and shaping the employee's behavior as close to the job as you can. In the actual cases that follow, we'll see that this strategy becomes a frequent guideline.

Again, these limitations should in no way promote a feeling of impotence or futility in the managerial role. The Emery Air Freight experience shows that within these limits there is still a great deal of room for maneuverability and successful results.

8

Motivational Style and Power

COUNTLESS dissertations have been written about the kind of traits and behaviors a good manager should have. Any introductory management course talks about the art of management, and about the job of management. If we distill all of this advice, two major themes emerge.

First, the personality and the style of the manager contribute to a subtle and important dimension in interpersonal effectiveness. Second, the formal and, more importantly, the informal use of power is the core of any leadership role. Without power, and the style to use it, the manager is a nonentity. We shall consider each of these factors in detail as they relate to motivation.

The Power Problem

The middle manager is in a peculiar power position. The role of top management is clear; it is responsible for policy, planning, and long-term, broad perspective problem solving. The role of the workers is clear: to fulfill the job requirements by doing the work. But the role of the middle managers is not at all clear. What *do* they do? There is no standard answer to this question because their organizational power position depends on what the people who have real power decide to delegate.

If, in the delegation process, the middle manager is given less authority than responsibility, he is put in a weak power position because the boss hasn't really given up anything. As a result, delegation is incomplete. Graphically, it would look like Figure 10. Since the authority delegated falls short of responsibility, the section represented by the broken line may actually revert back to the boss.

From the standpoint of motivation, the middle manager in this situation cannot help but feel like an External who has little control of rewards and punishments. This would present considerable problems at the lower levels of the organization, but among middle managers who actually may be Internals, the problems generated by this lack of power are enormous.

Figure 10. Incomplete delegation.

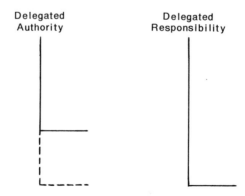

Multiply this powerlessness several times and you then have the motivational perspective of the middle-level *staff* employee who is much more of a peripheral power figure than the middle manager.

The importance of power, or rather the lack of it, can be demonstrated through an analogy to clinical psychology. We might say that depression represents a kind of opposite of positive motivation. A movement led by the psychologist Martin Seligman explains depression as the result of a person's believing that nothing he does has any effect on his life situation. That is, the individual believes that rewards and punishments occur *independently* of what he does. (In our terms this person would be an extreme External.)

Seligman calls this effect "learned helplessness." It can be produced experimentally in laboratory dogs that are given electric shocks in a cage from which they cannot escape. When the dogs are then placed in a cage in which they could escape the shocks by jumping over a small barrier, they fail to respond to the opportunity. Yet dogs that have not been exposed to the first cage easily learn to avoid the shocks in the second by jumping the barrier.

Many employees are conditioned into learned helplessness, and then even when a problem arises that they can easily solve, they seem to make no effort. Listen for this feeling; it is reflected in statements like "I'm blocked no matter what I try to do" or "You just can't do anything right around here." Much of the problem comes down to feelings of lack of power.

Distributive Justice

For the manager, either personally or in dealing with employees, the answer to this problem does not rest with simply getting or giving more rewards; it means the recipient should have a feeling of earning those rewards. This kind of feeling is often termed the *principle of distributive justice.* Distributive justice is the balance between investments and rewards. For example:

Investments	Rewards
Skills	Pay
Effort	Recognition
Education	Promotion

If employees perceive that their investments outweigh their rewards, they will feel cheated and will not be motivated. If they feel their rewards outweigh their investments, they will feel powerless from a personal perspective and will not be motivated. You see, in either situation the employees feel that what they do doesn't make any difference. Let us never believe that a giveaway program is the answer to motivation problems; nor is the answer never to give rewards. Rather, the key is a balance between giving and earning.

As usual, there is one complicating factor to this principle of distributive justice. Since it is the perception of the individual that counts, his idea of a balance between investments and rewards may be very different from someone else's. So, if an employee believes that X amount of effort should earn Y amount of reward and his manager believes that the effort should be doubled to earn the reward, a conflict is almost certain. This is where the exertion of power comes in; it attempts to impose one perception of justice rather than another, and it doesn't always work.

One way to deal with this complication is through the kind of power the manager uses. Basically, power fits one of two general categories: (1) reward-and-coercive power and (2) referent power. The first type builds up the reward end of a justice distribution, and the second builds the investment end.

Reward-and-coercive power relates to all types of rewards and punishments the manager has available, from praise to pay to criticism to firing. The reward or punishment the manager actually chooses is often a consequence of the type and nature of the investments. Of course, this is what the term "contingent" means; it depends on the behavior. And it influences the behavior, but only if the behavior is related. In this way, its influence on investments is significant, but indirect.

Referent power is personal power, and it has two subcategories: modeling and expert influence. Modeling power is exerted when another person wants to behave in the same way as you. For one reason or another, he is attracted to your style and behavior either because he believes it will enhance his self-esteem and higher order needs, or because he feels it will lead to tangible rewards. This kind of power relates directly to behavior (investments) and indirectly to rewards. Expert power is the power a person exerts by virtue of his special knowledge, training, or ability. Expert power is part of the direct input into the investment side of the distribution system. These two types of referent power can be used to alleviate conflicts caused by too much or too little emphasis on the rewards side.

Democratic Power

A widely reported potential solution to the problem of motivation and power has been the concept of industrial democracy. In his book *Job Power*, David Jenkins develops a thesis in favor of industrial democracy by maintaining that the alternative would mean fostering the further "evolution of the antiwork syndrome."[1] Here is his position.

First of all, industrial democracy is not just "industrial"; it applies to all types of organizations. It is not profit-sharing since that involves the distribution of money not power. And it isn't well represented by trade unionism either because unions only set guidelines and limits; they don't manage the organization.

Ideally, "industrial democracy" means control of the organization by the people who do the work. In some situations it may involve ownership, but that isn't its key feature. It must allow the workers to make decisions concerning general management of the organization. For example, election of supervisors to a limited rotating tenure incorporates the equalitarian

[1]*Job Power: Blue and White Collar Democracy,* Garden City, N.Y., Doubleday, 1973.

approach. Worker groups could make decisions about wages, prices, and production. To many people, this may sound like the Marxist argument against the hierarchy in capitalist organizations. It is, but this argument isn't necessarily anti-American.

Americans pride themselves on their governmental democracy—"consent by the governed"—and yet our corporate government is quite different.

Organizational decision making does not depend upon the yearly stockholders meeting, and the monthly board of directors meeting is limited due to other director commitments. Besides, the chairman and CEO present (and often filter) many of the issues the board is asked to advise on. Thus, many corporate empires in this country have policy decisions made by a handful of senior executives. This may be quite effective, but it isn't democracy.

Most of us never feel a conflict over the differences between our governmental system, which we would go to war to defend, and our organizational system, which we go to work to every day. One of our reactions in support of our capitalist system is that if a person owns a company and pays people to work there, he has a right to tell them what to do. Implicitly, this position means placing property rights above human rights. However, the employee agrees to give up certain rights in return for certain rewards or benefits.

Well, what precisely does this have to do with motivation? Power is an intricate part of the concept of motivation. Based on the locus of control approach toward rewards and punishments, and research like Seligman's on learned helplessness, we know that the feeling of having the power to reach a goal controls the *strength* of the motivation. Again, as is so often the case, this is not the whole answer.

Something Worth Doing

Recently, Arnold Tannenbaum of the University of Michigan's Institute for Social Research studied managers and workers in

Italy, Israel, Yugoslavia, Austria, and the United States.[2] He found that informal worker participation was highest in the Israeli kibbutz plants and lowest in the Italian factories, where the bosses were tough autocrats. Worker participation was second highest among Yugoslav workers, with U.S. workers a close third. Within the top three countries, however, the formal or informal system did not significantly affect worker satisfaction as much as did *job level* in the organization. In all cases, the bosses reported higher job satisfaction and more chances to do their own thing.

This study, and others like it, indicate that there is an additional factor to motivation that must be added to power. *What one has power to do must be worth doing;* that is, the perceived rewards and punishments must be of value. The power that the supervisor has to control insignificant working conditions can't compare to the power to set policy, change facilities, handle budgets, and influence lives that senior management has. That's why senior managers work 60-hour weeks. They have power that to them is highly significant.

This element of significance accounts for the moderate success of job enrichment programs. The enrichment literature asserts that job content changes are always vertical, not just more of the same-level task. Basically, what this means is that the organizational significance or importance of the new job is higher than the old one. What job enrichment programs don't always adequately consider is the enrichment of power along with enrichment of the job itself. The two don't go together automatically.

Perhaps an objection could be raised concerning the broad applicability of the desire for power. Are there people who don't want power? Maybe, but I don't think so; at least not the kind of power we speak of here. Locus of control power doesn't have to involve bossing people around or, in the reverse, never being dependent on others. It does mean, however, that what

---

[2]"Pecking Order, Capitalist and Communist Style," *Psychology Today,* September 1975.

action you choose to take will make some difference. Thus, a healthy dependency means people believe they have potential power, but they choose not to use it. It's when they don't want to be dependent and find they haven't the power to control their fate that learned helplessness takes over.

Also, power over oneself as a *level* of power is quite different from control over others. Even the most unambitious worker does not wish to view effort as meaningless. Even the most conditioned assembly line zombies like to believe they are being paid because they work. Even the established welfare recipient rationalizes that the assistance is somehow justified and deserved. As power and its perceived significance increase so does the motivation to exercise it. Why? Because it's worth doing, and your own actions can do it.

If there is any kind of a formula, this is it: *Power is the ability to generate, through your own actions, the rewards and punishments worth striving for.* This may sound simple, but remember: (1) There are all kinds of rewards and punishments, intrinsic and extrinsic, for all kinds of people; (2) setting up the conditions for *instrumental behavior* is not easy, and pretending that one technique will do the trick is a myth.

Work Values and Managerial Style

Perhaps the single most significant factor influencing the *effectiveness* of power over others is style. This is particularly true in terms of referent power because it is basically personal influence. Ideal leadership involves power derived from competence (expert) and admiration (modeling). Managers who aren't aware of this ideal often attempt to exert brute force (positional power) to achieve personal power. This is basically a contradiction similar to demanding respect; if you have to demand it, you can't have it. More accurately, personal power *commands* respect through referent power.

Translating this distinction into styles of management implies the difference between *authoritarian* and *authoritative* managers. An authoritarian style is dogmatic, rigid, demanding, and uncompromising. It may be benevolent without sacrificing any authoritarianism, as in a benevolent dictatorship. An authoritative style, on the other hand, uses personal influence, outside input, expert knowledge, and final decision-making responsibility to exert power.

At first glance, we may all conclude that, like Mother's Day, authoritative styles are best, but this is not always true. It depends very much on the nature of the employees being supervised, that is, on their level of needs, based on our model. In some cases an authoritarian style works well.

In addition to the characteristics of need level, we can add another set of descriptive guidelines which help to identify the employee's needs. These guidelines, developed by Professor Clare Graves of Union College, are called *work values*. They attempt to categorize certain personality traits and characteristic behavior of any workforce. The listing is as follows:

I	II
Tribalistic	Manipulative
Egocentric	Sociocentric
Conformist	Existential

An employee with tribalistic work values would be best suited for easy, routine work. This person likes a boss who gives direct and explicit direction, sometimes through participation.

For the egocentric work-values person, there are two major requirements. The job must pay well, and people must not be a hassle. The boss for this type of person must be tough and unintimidated.

The person with conformist work values derives security from well-defined rules and regulations. There is also a feeling that everyone else should follow the rules, and it becomes very upsetting to this person if they don't.

The manipulative work-values person likes a job that is varied and provides for opportunities to get ahead. This is the value system most often associated with managers. There is a good deal of political understanding on the part of this person.

Sociocentric work values include an emphasis of the importance of the work group and its common goals. The individual with these values is often concerned with broader organizational perspectives. Consumer advocates, political leaders, and executives often have some of the sociocentric traits (or, at least, they should have).

Finally, the existential values involve concern with the job and its problems above and beyond money or prestige. For instance, professional research and development people would share many of these values.

You will notice how nicely work values are separated into two columns labeled I and II. These correspond well to our model in Chapter 2. The first three work values involve External, Theory X assumption, low n Achievers, while the second three easily fit Internals, Theory Y assumption, high n Achievers.

Furthermore, the two categories of work values imply different power styles. Column I fits well with an *authoritarian* style, and II is better adapted to an *authoritative* style.[3]

An Example of Stylistic Power

One of my favorite illustrations of managerial style is the following letter:

Executive Mansion
Washington
January 26, 1863

Major General Hooker
General:

I have placed you at the head of the Army of the Potomac. Of course, I have done this upon what appear to me to be sufficient reasons. And yet I think it best for you to know

---

[3]Vincent S. Flowers et al., *Managerial Values for Working*, an AMA survey report, New York, AMACOM, 1975, p. 15.

that there are some things in regard to which, I am not quite satisfied with you. I believe you to be a brave and skillful soldier, which, of course, I like. I also believe you do not mix politics with your profession, in which you are right. You have confidence in yourself, which is a valuable, if not an indispensable quality. You are ambitious, which, within reasonable bounds, does good rather than harm. But I think that during Gen. Burnside's command of the Army, you have taken counsel of your ambition, and thwarted him as much as you could, in which you did a great wrong to the country, and to a most meritorious and honorable brother officer. I have heard, in such a way as to believe it, of your recently saying that both the Arms and the Government need a Dictator. Of course, it was not for this, but in spite of it, that I have given you the command. Only generals who gain success, can set up dictators. What I now ask of you is military success, and I will risk the dictatorship. The government will support you to the utmost of its ability, which is neither more nor less than it has done and will do for all commanders. I much fear that the spirit which you have aided to infuse into the Army, of criticizing their Commander, and withholding confidence from him, will now turn upon you. I shall assist you as far as I can, to put it down. Neither you, nor Napoleon, if he were alive again, could get any good out of an army, while such a spirit prevails in it.

And now, beware of rashness. Beware of rashness, but with energy, and sleepless vigilance, go forward, and give us victories.

> Your very truly,
> A. Lincoln

At first this seems like an ordinary memo issuing some sort of directive not very different from the hundreds of "distributions" that you get each month. However, a closer examination of the structure and the style of this letter reveals a great deal.

Structurally, it appears at first glance to use the "sandwich" technique of praise-criticism-praise. This, of course, is a format commonly used by many managers as a shaping device, but it usually doesn't work. It doesn't work because the shaping is too obviously interpreted as manipulation. You will recall that in the Greenspoon shaping experiments, some of the subjects who became aware of the technique exhibited reactance—a rebellion against the shaping. Suppose you call an employee into your office and begin by telling him what a good job he's done. Just reverse the roles for a moment and you'll see how obvious your shaping is. If *your* boss calls you in and starts out that way, what's your first reaction? "My God, what have I done now!" You're way ahead, anticipating the shaping, and it's then exposed for what it is—a poor attempt at using power.

Thus, the sandwich approach is basically a style that announces insecurity and reluctance to use power. From what we know about our bosses, and perhaps about ourselves, this may be a major leadership problem. Under these conditions, the employee may be able to shape the boss because of the signals a style such as this gives off. No wonder, then, that employee motivation is channeled into little shaping games instead of organizational objectives.

From what we know about Lincoln, fear of using power was not one of his problems. We can see from the letter that after a few statements of fact, the point is made: "I am not quite satisfied with you." So it really isn't the sandwich technique he is using.

The style of this letter is not authoritarian so much as it is authoritative. Lincoln reminds me of the special kind of leader who can be critical of you throughout most of a face-to-face meeting, yet you walk out saying, in effect, "Thank you very much." Lincoln makes it very clear that he knows what is going on in terms of the General's ambition. Actually, if I received a letter like this, I would feel quite threatened, and yet he doesn't make threats in the letter—just the opposite: He gives advice, and even support. If by the General's own doing he gets into trouble, what will Lincoln's position be? Well, most managers would say something like, "I told you so. You made your bed, now lie in it." There is a certain satisfaction in putting down someone who has not responded to your efforts toward shaping. Perhaps Lincoln had this feeling, but in the letter he rises above it, assuring Hooker that should he get into trouble, "The government will support you to the utmost of its ability." I wonder how many of us would do that for our people.

Finally, Lincoln's style is soaked with self-confidence. He says that the General is in no position to become a dictator unless he is promoted and successful. Between the lines, Lincoln is telling him, "Be successful. I want that; I'll risk it, because then when you and I compete head to head, I'll win."

The last sentence is almost inspirational: ". . . with energy, and sleepless vigilance, go forward, and give us victories." If I were the General, after reading this letter, I'd be pretty sure that the President had my number and that he knew the score, and for that he would have my respect as a leader.

So, what's the point here? Certainly every manager is not a Lincoln, nor needs to be. But the point is that managerial style is a subtle, almost ephemeral, quality that goes beyond the administering of rewards and punishments. Style is the art of management and motivation. We are only now starting to identify it and recognize its importance. It will be some time before we know how to teach it.

9
Situational
Principles I

Training Managers

One of the most interesting assignments I have ever had was a training and consulting task for the consortium of oil companies building the trans-Alaska pipeline. The uniqueness of this job was twofold. First of all, it was in Alaska, which in many ways is like no other part of the country, and secondly, it was with an organization that was supposed to do something that hadn't been done before and then complete itself out of existence.

On a project that costs about $7 billion, whatever problems average construction organizations would have can be multiplied several times. For instance, purchasing, maintaining, and controlling 4,000 pieces of equipment and indirectly coordinating the work of some 19,000 employees are big jobs. Compared to other organizations, the growth of the project was almost instant. Even though there was considerable engineering lead time, there was very little organizational preparation time. Right from the beginning, there was a "shoot from the hip" attitude throughout the organization.

These characteristics made for not only organizational problems but also benefits. I would like to identify briefly the employee needs as an example of how to assess an organization based on our model. There were basically three groups of employees: managers, office employees, and union employees.

The union employees were supervised not directly, but through subcontractors. At the time I was there, the lowest laborers' salary was $9.50 an hour. They worked 12 hours a day, seven days a week, for nine weeks and then got a week off. The primary motivation on the job was money first, adventure second.

The office employees were clerks and typists located mainly in Anchorage. They worked shorter hours than the union people and were paid about the same as in any organization except for a cost of living differential. Their primary motivation was to have a job.

The managers were usually from the owner oil companies. Many of them had been on oil construction projects before. They received a considerable wage incentive based on their base salary. Their primary motivations were money, challenge, and promotions—not necessarily in that order. There were also managers who were hired directly by the consortium.

I generally found that the level of need for achievement was higher for all three groups than for comparable employees in other organizations. The sense of accomplishment and the feeling of pride about the pipeline itself were apparant particularly among the managers. Comments like "This is the largest privately financed project ever attempted. It is second in scope and technical difficulty only to the space program" were typical expressions of this attitude, which could be, and often was, used as the motivation behind extra commitments of time and effort.

This sense of awe at the project only went so far, however, and its impact depended on the work values and need level of the employee. In this regard, I noticed a great deal of *temporary functional autonomy*—that is, some employees tried to convince themselves that the intrinsic goals of the project were sufficient justification for dedicated performance. Since this effort was somewhat artificial, there was often a kind of slipping back to old values.

At times the reinforcements for not working outweighed the rewards for working, to the frustration of management:

> Some of these office clerks won't show up for two or three days because they've decided to go off fishing, or hunting, or camping. When they come back, they act like this is perfectly normal behavior. That's the way it is up here, and it makes it hard to get anything done.

It was my impression that most of the executives were basically Internals who felt that they had substantial control in achieving the long-range goals of the project. The managers and office employees had certain External traits, particularly in terms of their tangible contributions to building the pipeline. This attitude was reflected in comments similar to this one: "We'll diddle around down here, and they'll build the pipeline. Then we'll all go home."

This is a classic problem between executive levels and lower managerial levels. The executives have one form or another of either functional autonomy or intangible goals, and they encounter all sorts of communication, motivation, and performance problems when they try to translate their motives down through the organization. They are motivated in one way, and for some reason they think that everyone can or should be motivated in the same way. This is a myth.

They can shape behavior through direct reinforcement and through modeling, but most executives don't take the time to do a functional analysis of the needs of the manager or em-

ployee they're trying to reach. They either attempt to impose
their needs or they underestimate and "offer down"—that is,
they become condescending and manipulative.

Now, in Alaska where the organizational structure is new
and constantly changing, this disparity between one motivation level and another is magnified. There isn't the communication time to mutually assess the kinds of needs and motives
that can build trust. Everyone is new and insecure, so everyone regresses into lower levels and patterns of behavior to be
safe, and performance quality suffers. Top management sees
this happening and wants to change it. It calls in its personnel
people and asks for an analysis. The report that comes back
says, from personnel's point of view, the managers and supervisors have too many people problems. Let's train them. We'll
call in the "people people."

This is the point where I've usually made my entrance.
What I find is technically qualified people who have been
promoted to managers. Sometimes they have interesting personalities; usually they're dull. Sometimes they have a strong
human relations orientation; usually they're insecure and un-
aware. Sometimes they're emotionally expressive and mature;
usually they have an adolescent mentality. The training programs are two days, three days, maybe a week.

Whenever you're thrust into these situations, you have this
sinking feeling that you should have been a plumber or something. Some of the participants have to be there and they already know all the answers, none of which relate to their own
behavior since *they* aren't the problem. Yet as you listen to the
group, you find there are some technicians-turned-managers
who realize they don't have all the skills of a good manager.
They want to acquire tools and learn techniques that will help
them improve the performance of their employees and in turn
make their own jobs more enjoyable. They're very aware of
the alienation and counterproductivity that exist in organizations, and they want to make an effort to change the image of
management.

This is the picture of the Alaska situation. We reached some managers and gave them new knowledge, and yet there were others who wasted their time because they didn't have ears to hear what was being said. By the time I left, I had heard many reports of interactions between managers who had been through the training and were exchanging applications of the same principles I've presented in this book. This was partly due to an unusually wise decision by personnel and senior management to send managers from all levels through the training. This avoided the common trainee complaint "I wish my boss were hearing this stuff." It is my belief that this training is a proper step in the *evolutionary* process of developing a manager.

The Incentive Problem

I recall one situation where a department head used early quitting time as an incentive. This was against company policy, and the general manager came down hard on the department head. Here is the story: A large department store operation was having particularly difficult problems with two departments, shipping and floor ticketing. They had high turnover and absenteeism rates, they were constantly failing to meet deadlines, and there were frequent complaints to personnel about management rules and regulations.

Samuels, the general manager, decided to promote a young two-year-college graduate to the position of department head in ticketing after the old supervisor resigned. Brown, the new supervisor, had been working for the department as an assistant supervisor for about a year, so this seemed like a logical choice. Almost immediately, the ticketing department started to improve. There was a decrease in complaints from the floor about improper ticketing, and personnel felt that grievances about management had decidedly declined. All in all, it seemed like the new supervisor was doing a good job.

After about two straight months of steady improvement in ticketing, the head of the shipping department came to Samuels and said that he was having all kinds of problems because the ticketing people were quitting work 15 to 20 minutes before the end of the day and the shipping people felt cheated. It was getting more and more difficult for the shipping supervisor to enforce this rule when it was being so flagrantly violated next door.

Samuels called Brown into his office the next day and asked him about the early quitting time. Brown said that after a couple of days on the job, he told his people that if their performance improved he would set up informal quotas that would give them extra time at the end of the day to freshen up, talk, and relax.

Samuels was very upset. He told Brown that the employees had adequate breaks during the day, and that the store policy was set up for a reason. Not only was this new practice arbitrary, but it was creating problems. And besides, supervisors didn't have the power to set policy. Therefore, Brown was to withdraw the early quitting time incentive immediately.

The outcome? The ticketing department slumped back into its old performance problems, and six months after Samuel's decision, Brown quit.

Several points about this case come to mind. The most obvious is Samuels' human relations technique in ordering company policy to be restored and enforced. In this regard, even the sandwich approach would have been better than his method. From Brown's perspective, it couldn't help but be interpreted as punishment, and for what? Well, in a way it was punishment for what Samuels considered bad judgment, but Brown could easily interpret it as punishment for managerial initiative. You will recall that the law of effect says that punishing a behavior decreases the probability that the behavior will be repeated.

Suppose we extend this first observation on down the organizational line. There was the danger that when Brown withdrew this incentive it would be perceived as punishment by the employees in the ticketing department. As punishment for what? His mistake? Maybe, but there is the possibility they would view it as punishment for improved performance.

Another question that must be asked concerns the efficacy of company policy. If this violation improved performance, then why not change company policy? After all, the employees are not really being paid for time; rather, they're paid for what they do. While it is true that company policy often loses its real point, this was not the case here. Let us examine the nature of the incentive in order to see this point.

The time off may well have been functioning here as a hygiene factor. It didn't affect the content of the work; it was a condition of work. In a way, Brown had backed himself into a corner, since these factors go back to zero, and you then must raise the absolute level to achieve a relative gain. The coffee break was once a privilege given by management as a kind of specific recognition, but today it's considered a right and is incorporated in most union contracts. This 15-minute incentive has the potential to mushroom to 25, and then 30, and so on. Therefore, this was a poor hygiene incentive to select because relative gains could only erode the time available for job performance. Because of this, the company policy had to remain intact.

The next point for consideration is how Samuels might have withdrawn the incentive, which was clearly against a valid company policy, without negative repercussions. Precipitous removal would be (and actually was) perceived as punishment; thus, a substitution would seem warranted. The work values of the employees were probably tribalistic, so, at least at this point, substituting a hygiene factor for a motivator possibly would not be as effective as substituting another hygiene or low satiation factor. Samuels could have resorted to a menu of factors such as were discussed previously. In addition, he would have had to evaluate the desirability of shaping the substitution gradually or imposing the changes immediately.

Here, the Premack principle would be something to consider, as would the idea of presenting a couple of acceptable menu items for participative group consideration.

Actually, Samuels would be dealing with two problems—one concerning the use of a poor incentive, and the other the shipping department's performance—and one solution would not be likely to work for both problems.

On-the-Job Associations

In general, and aside from the above case, there is a potential paradox in comparing the kind of rewards used in organizations and their associative value. Psychologists maintain that the law of effect ("Rewarding a behavior increases the probability that the behavior will be repeated") works because the reward is *associated* with the behavior that immediately precedes it. The closer this bonding, the more effective the association value. Well, there are very few organizational rewards that can actually be used on the job. You don't spend your paycheck at work; you don't use your fringe benefits at work. Even incentives like vacations and time off, as in the last case, are attractive precisely because they mean less time on the job. If so many rewards are associated with off-the-job activities and opportunities, *no wonder people don't want to come to work.*

That's why strategies such as job enrichment become so popular. They affect on-the-job behavior and rewards. Now, the argument might be made that the rewards that are enjoyed *off* the job can only be earned *on* the job and the more opportunities to earn them, the stronger the motivation on the job. This is true, but only up to a point. If the job is only a means to an end, it is viewed as having little intrinsic value as an end in itself. This is exactly what functional autonomy is *not.* Our conclusion: *Off-the-job rewards can be opposed to the encouragement of functional autonomy on the job.*

Functional Autonomy and Modeling

In an effort to present an ideal role model, many executives attempt to impose their values and work standards on their people. Leadership by example is not easy. Here is an example of how it can backfire.

Richard Locastro is vice president of a medium-size manufacturing and service organization. He is 40 years old and was labeled early in his career as "a bright young executive on the move."

A go-getter, Locastro is usually the first to get to work each morning, generally arriving by 7 A.M. His employees, whom he always refers to as "my team," don't arrive until 9 o'clock. By that time, Locastro has accomplished a great deal, and he often makes this point clear to his people. Not only does he arrive early, but he also always stays late, so he thinks nothing of calling a management meeting at 4:30 or 5. Also, he works every Saturday and measures the dedication of his secretary and managers by their willingness to do likewise.

Most of the managers, aware of the need to demonstrate enthusiasm and commitment, comply by coming in one or two Saturdays a month. Aware of resentment, Locastro says from time to time that no one is forced, or even pressured, to work Saturdays. Yet those who come in *every* Saturday receive considerable praise and reinforcement from him. The others feel that this recognition is unfair, especially since many of them feel they owe their families at least part of their time. But their real complaint centers around their lack of accomplishment and their need to cater to Locastro's ego.

What is this case all about? Well, basically, for one reason or another, Locastro has achieved a certain degree of functional autonomy in his job, or so it seems. His managers don't share it and he can't understand that, so he tries to shape their behavior by using external praise and recognition when they act like him. They resent such tactics as unfair manipulation, while he sees his behavior as offering a model for leadership development. It won't work.

Compliance is not motivation. Forcing functional autonomy is like demanding respect. Either effort is at odds with the process by which it develops. To repeat, you can't demand respect since, in its genuine form, respect is a voluntary *attitude.* In the same vein, functional autonomy can only be encouraged indirectly and not forced through the will of another person.

Remember that functional autonomy is attached to specific need levels, and it is unrealistic to shape for autonomy on a level where the needs are not yet felt. Locastro is trying to get his managers to internalize needs that they don't feel. He must first reach them on their achievement level and then encourage vertical movement through the enrichment of the job. The jobs can be enriched through content and power. Motivation to stay longer will follow as the night follows the day. Simply, they don't now have an *autonomous reason* to stay on the job, and *external* praise or evaluation apprehension will not produce one. In fact, it may prevent the development of autonomy because it serves as an excuse or substitute that encourages horizontal movement.

From the description of Locastro, you may have labeled him "a benevolent autocrat." He has a parental style and demands tremendous personal loyalty, and he gets it from some of his managers, but I would guess that they are not going to be outstanding performers in the organization. They don't have the autonomy to take risks, be creative, assert initiatives, or even provide dissent for Locastro's decision-making responsibilities.

I would recommend the following stance for Locastro. Firstly, he should shape into each manager's job more meaningful content and more managerial power. He should *encourage* them to go home within the reasonable quitting times that have been set as company policy. This could leave them "hungry" to get to work the next day, especially with the new exciting course their jobs are taking. Finally, if he wants to be a model, he should make his dedication as inconspicuous as possible. He might even try to *hide* his extra working hours from his employees. This would reinforce, in their eyes, the autonomous nature of his dedication, since he would clearly be doing it not to impress or coerce them but for its own sake.

Like Locastro, too many executives are not as functionally autonomous as they would like to believe. Actually, they are rather insecure and, for this reason, need to make a grand production out of the fact that they are working above and beyond the petty external rewards, the gumdrops. But, in an almost parasitic fashion, they live off the reward of comparing themselves with others and seeing them react with resentful admiration. This is the old ego-massage trick, and it's used by too many executives who kid themselves about their insecurities.

Role Acceptance and Motivation

Sales and marketing are lifeblood functions in many organizations, and salespeople are among the most challenging, difficult, and satisfying to manage. Most have a high need for achievement, and while they demonstrate independence, social influence processes can significantly affect them as a group. The success of the sales meeting as a motivator attests to these unique characteristics, particularly those involved in field or "on the road" sales. It's true that not everyone can sell, and great sellers may be born not made, but good salespeople can be produced through the development efforts of management. The case that follows demonstrates a fairly typical motivation problem among new salespeople or among those in sales who have lost their enthusiasm but not their competence.

Harold Simmons had joined the company right out of college as a sales trainee. On all written exams, he demonstrated a high level of performance. His knowledge of sales techniques and company policy was excellent. In field training, he was well liked by all the salespeople he traveled with, and they reported that he devoted a good deal of time and effort to his job. He wanted to learn everything he could about sales, and he was completely open and honest. People enjoyed answering his questions; they considered him part of a new breed of employee that was clearly appreciated.

Harold was soon given his own territory, and sales management looked forward to his becoming one of its top salespeople in short order. However, his first sales report was very disappointing; there were declines in sales for nearly all products. This was a tough territory, but these results were not what the sales manager, Frank Carter, had expected.

When the figures for the second period came in, they were even slightly worse than for the first. Now Carter felt the situation needed to be investigated, so he went out into the field and talked with the various purchasing agents. Here was the picture: Harold was considered honest, reliable, even likable, but many people commented that he seemed very solemn and dragged out. He would come into their offices, say hello, run down the order sheet, ask if he could help, and then make his goodbyes and hurry out. In short, he never did anything but take orders.

Carter checked on some clients who had dropped the company's products before Harold was given the territory, and they said they had never seen the new man. Carter knew he had told Harold about these people. In fact, Carter had even made a list for Harold before assigning him to the field.

When Carter called Harold into the office, Harold was pretty upset and said he knew he was having trouble but couldn't seem to do anything about it. He wanted to do well, but often he couldn't help but see the situation from the point of view of the customer. Some of the promotional material was questionable, he felt, and some of the high-profit items he was told to push were no better than some of the lower-priced models. Finally, sometimes the territory seemed like more than he could handle, but he wasn't a quitter and he'd conquer it somehow.

Perhaps the first question here is, Why did Harold do so well as a trainee and then seem to fall on his face when given his own territory? Specifically, was he prepared to take on the autonomy and independence required by the job? In a way he was beyond it, and yet in another way he couldn't handle it.

His work values were probably oriented in a *sociocentric* direction; that is, he had concern for others and saw the broader picture from the ethical and moral point of view. Perhaps successful selling (without any pejorative meaning intended) requires more *manipulative* work values: the desire to see and take advantage of opportunities without necessarily being exploitative.

On a wider level, the college experience actually teaches young people to be excellent trainees, encourages them, almost, to be trainees all their lives. They learn to absorb material, to be enthusiastic and friendly—all under the guidance of leadership that sets the rules. Harold was only responding out on the job to the conditioning he had been subject to for most of his educational life. That's just what we would predict—why are managers so surprised when it happens?

Put differently, Harold was responding to a directed, almost programmed kind of shaping educationally; but occupationally *he* had to do the shaping, he had to be the shaper, not the subject, and he rejected the role because it was quite new and uncomfortable.

This apparent lack of enthusiasm can also occur in salespeople who have performed well in the past but are now in a slump. While many factors may be involved—such as boredom, other interests, or type of supervision—lack of confidence is a prime element. This is the emphasis at all sales rallies and pep talks. There is a "psyching up" process that must work if a person is going to be a good seller. This is equivalent to saying that the person must accept the role of being a *shaper*, and it requires a strong *Internal*-personality type.

Good sales training, then, must take individuals who have initially been selected as potential sellers and *shape their acceptance of the role*. For some people this will fail, and they belong in other jobs; for others it will enhance their *high need for achievement*, their *manipulative* needs, and their Internal natures.

In summary, then, the sales manager must be able to identify a problem like Harold's as one of *role conflict* and put the issue squarely on the table. The salesperson either (1) works on fitting the role, (2) changes his perception of the role, or (3) changes roles completely. The first alternative means adaptation that is deliberate, the second means subtle shaping by the manager, and the third means getting a different job.

10
Situational
Principles II

Role Definitions and Motivation

ONE of the major frustrations of a manager or employee who understands motivation can be the sense of powerlessness to change others in the organization. Especially if you're in a staff position, the influence you can exert may be quite limited. Not accepting this as a limitation can get you into some real dilemmas, as this next example indicates.

Here was the case as Ron Kaussner explained it to me. He was hired to fill a new job as assistant to Dr. Clifford Grazier, the director of the research and development department of a large chemicals company.

After about six months in the new position, Ron felt he had gotten to know everyone pretty well and was getting along fine. One afternoon, over coffee, he heard that one of their best research assistants, Debbie Truex, was seriously thinking about quitting. Apparently, Debbie's boss, Dr. Schwab, was giving her a lot of extra routine work. She was finding it difficult to complete all of her assignments, which she had to do in order to be evaluated positively, and she also found the additional work dull and unsatisfying. Debbie had asked for a clerical assistant, but the request was turned down.

At this point, Ron was unsure of just what to do. He didn't really know if Schwab was aware of Debbie's desire to quit. Although technically Schwab was highly competent, he did have a reputation for being autocratic. Ron and he hadn't hit it off too well, and right from the start Schwab had made it perfectly clear he thought an "assistant to" position was a needless expense. Now, Ron was apprehensive about speaking to Dr. Grazier because that might cause Debbie embarrassment, and he didn't want to be regarded as a spy, anyway. What could he do?

First, let's look at the organization chart (Figure 11) so we can visualize these various roles and relationships. Keep in mind that an "assistant to" is a very different position from an assistant. As an "assistant to," Ron is an aide and has no authority over the line organization except what is explicitly delegated. An assistant, on the other hand, is the number two person in the organization and has all the authority of a line position. Thus, given Ron's staff role, his direct intervention as an authority is not possible.

Figure 11. Organization chart for the Debbie Truex case.

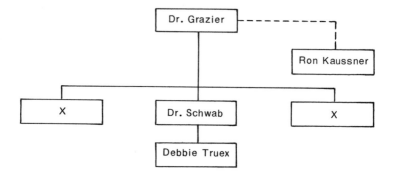

An important question as to the extent of his responsibility in this situation arises. After all, he is not responsible for the motivational problems of the department. Maybe he should just keep his mouth shut. Since he can't do anything personally, he may only stand to lose ground by attempting to intervene.

The other perspective, however, is that as a part of the organization he does have an implied responsibility to try to the best of his abilities to improve the department's performance and cooperation. If he could prevent a needless loss of a competent employee, he should at least make some sort of effort. But what kind of effort?

He could go to Grazier and apprise him of the situation, or he could go to Schwab on behalf of Debbie, or he could go to Debbie and tell her to go to Grazier, or tell her to go back again to Schwab. Whatever he decides, he must have his role and the long-term effects in proper perspective.

His primary responsibility is to Grazier, his boss, but should he present to him what is at this point only a rumor? Shouldn't he get the whole story first? This is one approach. He can go to Debbie and find out the details. If the rumor proves to be well founded, he can approach Grazier and tell him what the story is, and let him take it from there.

However, in light of Ron's unclear role in this matter, my first choice would be for him to go to Schwab. Ron is not, as I see it, responsible for *vertical motivation problems*, which this case represents. That is, and should be, the responsibility of line management. Without even checking out the rumor, he could approach Schwab and tell him that he heard that Debbie was unhappy, that he didn't want to get involved, and that it would be up to Schwab to do what he saw fit.

What would be the implications of this course of action? Well, Schwab might throw Ron out of the office and then go out and fire Debbie for making him look bad by complaining to everyone in the department. I think he would not be likely to do that, however. Initially, he may resent Ron's "one-up-manship," but it is also possible that he could perceive Ron as one who has done him a favor by preventing a resignation that could be embarrassing. He may, in time, even come to the conclusion that Ron is making an effort to have him look *good* in Grazier's eyes.

This particular case opens up a broader issue in organizations. Staff people should not get embroiled in line problems. When personnel becomes the crutch for managers who cannot motivate their people with the right combination of power and style, the net result is weak leadership. Of course, staff are there to serve an advisory and support function, but they should not be an excuse or a scapegoat for management's lack of functionally autonomous behavior.

I have seen too often the attitude that personnel is in charge of selection of employees, human relations, and motivation. This is a serious myth that leads us to polarized leadership. A personnel department should exist only to do paperwork and distribute information. *Every good manager should be a walking personnel department.* Thus, no staff person should get between managers and head-to-head contact with their people.

Now, you can easily respond to such a position statement by saying that it's unrealistic, and that most managers don't have the interpersonnal competence to be as autonomous as is suggested here. Maybe, but then why aren't they as qualified in this area as they should be, and whose fault is it? As I see it, the responsibility rests squarely on the manager's shoulders. No one in personnel can be a surrogate for the human side of management while the manager deals with the technical side. Unfortunately, this dichotomy has been the trend up to now, but it's not working.

To Motivate or to Accommodate

At some point, every manager is faced with an employee problem that is a source of irritation, but it isn't the kind of problem that you want blown up out of proportion. Let me cite a case in sales and marketing that could occur just as easily in any department.

Sid Williams, the sales manager, related the following

story. He had been very proud of luring Bob Tabone away from one of their major competitors about nine months ago. Bob was a top performer; in fact, he had been taking away customers from them for some time, but the offer of a better commission and fringe benefits had finally brought him, and his customers, to the company.

There was never any question that Bob knew the territory or that he could sell. So Williams only talked to him at the outset about the different paperwork procedures Bob would have to know. He stressed the fact that they were a large company and had a lot of different kinds of orders coming in. As a result they had to be coded and processed accurately. Bob said that wasn't any problem as far as he was concerned.

For the first couple of months there were no problems with Bob, and actually he had been steadily increasing the sales volume of the territory. Then accounting called Williams to complain that Bob wasn't sending in his expense account every week but was saving them up for four or five weeks, and that really screwed up its record-keeping. Williams talked to Bob about it and was reassured that the time interval between his expense reports would be reduced.

Two weeks later, Williams got a complaint from the order processing supervisor that Bob's handwriting was so bad that the clerks couldn't read the quantities, model numbers, or shipping instructions. Williams called Bob in.

This time Bob exploded and accused Williams of wanting not a seller but some kind of a pencil pusher. He said that all his efforts were directed toward selling and not paperwork. Finally, he asked the manager if he wanted a few superneat orders or a lot of not-so-neat ones, and left the office.

In a way this is a small problem, and yet it's creating some significant turmoil. This type of behavior is not unusual among talented and independent-minded people, and at times managers must acknowledge the value of autonomous behavior. This problem is common among salespeople, researchers, and creative spirits. Thus, there is value in it, and yet a manager still has to run a department and control the efforts of the staff.

In this particular case, Williams can choose to shape Bob's behavior with subtle rewards and punishments. He might direct that any paperwork irregularities generated by Bob be referred to him, and he might then confront Bob face to face on each violation for a short period of time. This may be enough pressure to correct the carelessness. He might also set down firm regulations about paperwork processes and institute strong rewards and punishments to put teeth into the policy. It might even be worth an extra percent of commission or a commission decrease. While any shaping technique can work well on "picky" problems, there is also another possibility.

Williams might decide to work around Bob. It could be that a *system improvement* would help all the salespeople. Maybe a preprinted order form would be the answer, or one clerical assistant to process the paperwork for all the salespeople, or a telephone system, or a tape recorder. These changes might even expedite order times and minimize errors, thus increasing customer satisfaction.

Many managers have a gut reaction against special treatment for individuals. They feel that such an approach is unprofessional and smacks of favoritism. But there is also the matter of priorities. Giving up five dollars to make a hundred is not a sacrifice; nor is it special privilege. Overall contribution has to be considered. If Bob's paperwork problems are less important than his sales record, maybe he is worth working around.

So, in this situation you have three choices: (1) Shape Bob's behavior and you'll see the problem disappear, but you might also see sales drop or Bob leave. (2) Change the system to affect everyone and thereby solve the problem with Bob. (3) Put up with the problem based on Bob's sales performance.

I see the second alternative as the most promising. Keep in mind that this approach is not directly motivational; it is organizational. Again, by attributing too much significance to the need to change the person, especially in a minor matter, we could disrupt the performance we're now getting. Tinkering should be reserved for more meaningful motivation problems.

Every manager should be required to take a pledge of non-abuse: "I will use motivational power sparingly and properly." Repeat 20 times!

Assessing and Identifying Motives

Trying to evaluate the potential of employees is one of a manager's most difficult problems. Weighing a person's motives against job requirements is an important element in the selection process. Identification of motives is also a judgment and can only be an estimation of probabilities. I think this next situation illustrates this well.

Jim Antonio, a section manager for a large Wall Street brokerage house, has to decide on a successor to one of his unit supervisors, who has recently resigned. In line for the promotion are two senior clearing clerks—we'll call them Mary and George. Mary gets along very well with her co-workers and seems quite capable of assuming a leadership role. In fact, she has informally expressed an interest in supervision in the past. George, on the other hand, is introverted and shy. He comes to the office each day, does his job, and goes home, usually without saying very much to his colleagues. Both people are technically competent, and their seniority is just about equal, each having been hired a year ago in a reorganization effort.

Jim feels that Mary would be his first choice except for one factor. Her husband is a salesman for a large computer company and has already been transferred to four different cities in the last ten years. Whoever got the promotion would have to go through a fairly involved training program.

Now Jim is aware of recent governmental regulations on discrimination. He knows also that it's a no-no to come right out and ask Mary, "You're a candidate for the job, but is your husband going to be transferred again soon?" The human rights people would cut out his vital organs for that one. Yet he also knows he can refuse her the job and be on solid ground, with George's qualifications being equal.

Basically, Jim's dilemma can be segregated into some known factors and some unknown factors about each person. He knows that both are technically competent, that Mary is outgoing and likable, and that George is shy and introverted. He doesn't know if either of them will make a good supervisor, or if either of them will leave.

What he is really trying to do is assess motives, and translate that assessment into predictions about performance. This case is somewhat different from the others in that it involves the manager not in an attempt to increase motivation but in a matching process between person and job.

Thus, Jim's first step should be to evaluate the costs of Mary's leaving versus the benefits of her being a good supervisor while she is there. Alongside this must go the outcome of assessing George's introversion as a crucial factor in his becoming a good supervisor. After all, supervision is not necessarily a popularity contest, and, besides, George may bloom out if given the proper opportunity. Mary seems more motivated for the job, but couldn't George's behavior be shaped in that direction too?

Is it possible that Jim wouldn't be in this position in the first place if he had planned and groomed a successor all along? Maybe, but there are two problems with the position such a question implies:

1. A growing, flexible organization cannot always allow itself the luxury of such advance planning because of the changing nature of the roles and responsibilities within the structure.

2. It isn't always a good idea, motivationally, to have a lot of crown princes walking around waiting to become kings.

It boils down to only one significant variable in this promotion problem: Which personality type is the better risk for a supervisory position? My inclination, which is not absolute, is to select Mary. She would require shaping primarily in the area of leadership. This would be more than enough for Jim to do. By hoping to shape George into a communicator who takes the initiative, Jim would simply be adding one more staff development task to his job as a manager.

11
A Broader Perspective

THIS chapter brings us around full circle from a general introduction, to theory, to practice, to specifics, and back to the general picture again.

Informal managers must be able to view from a wider vantage point than one set of circumstances if they ever hope to rise above their own situation. The trends and currents within our society eventually filter down to the one-to-one interactions that occur in our organizations.

To remain isolated and hope for immunity to the forces shaping our world has never worked in the past and does not serve us well in an ever shrinking world. Personally, I never underestimate my capacity for rationalizing uninvolvement. The standard rationale relates to the locus of control. Whenever I don't want to get involved in a potentially difficult situ-

ation, I become an External and develop a feeling of powerlessness over the matter, which in turn justifies my inaction.

The organizational psychologist and administrator Warren
Bennis relates an interesting story about inaction. When Nikita
Khrushchev, then Premier of the Soviet Union, visited New
York, he held a news conference and one of the questions submitted in writing asked what he, as a ranking government figure
even then, was doing during the atrocities of the Stalin years.
Khrushchev was livid with rage. He pounded on the lectern
and ordered whoever asked the question to stand up. The
room was dead silent, and no one stood up. After what seemed
like an infinite pause, Khrushchev stepped back and said
calmly, "That's what I was doing."

Our point is that while at times sitting back silently may be
justified through powerlessness, it can become a habit that per-
sists even after one attains a position of power. In fact, an argument could be made that it is only the powerless who stand up
to be heard, for the powerful have vested interests that keep
them glued to their chairs. You cannot justify your inaction toward change by claiming smallness of position.

Before you go running out to change the world, however,
in the light of what I've said about motivation, assessing trends
and patterns might be a wise place to start. From there, you
can plan your strategy.

Motivation and the Work Ethic

What can we realistically expect to be the outcome of our current motivation problems in organizations? My response centers on two issues: the work ethic and affluence.

What is the work ethic? We hear it discussed often, and it
is usually in the context of a debate about the young and about
the future of American industrial and economic growth. The
work ethic is a set of values. These values give importance to
certain types of behaviors including orderliness, punctuality,
success seeking, respect for rank and authority, and predicta-

bility. To some people today, these behaviors sound awfully dull.

There exist new values today that will grow in the future. These values represent a need to break out of the traditional Calvinist work ethic. Behaviors such as spontaneity, pleasure seeking, equality of rank, and unpredictability are becoming important. With these new values emerging, quite naturally, the work ethic sectors of our society have become concerned. They do not want to see the efforts and products of their labor disregarded and destroyed. Rest easy folks, it isn't going to happen—at least, not within the next few generations.

It is true that the values of the work ethic no longer have the overwhelming, blanketing impact and influence they once had, and organizations can no longer treat employees as if those values hadn't changed, but neither have the values been abandoned. They have been balanced and counterweighted through the development of the newer values of life.

The newer values, by the way, are not new at all, and in the past they have always played a part to a greater or lesser extent in defining the meaning of life. They have declined or risen with the cultural tide. It is my belief that they are on the rise again. However, I feel that their rise will not require a corresponding decline in work ethic values. Why not? Because of the taste of widespread affluence.

Affluence in terms of material and creature comforts has been a more or less direct spin-off of the work ethic. The drive behind technological and organizational development has allowed us to see many positive attacks on the vulgarities of the human condition. Advances in food production, medicine, and social structure are results of the work ethic that will not be forsaken.

Given the uncertain nature of world events, should our affluence be threatened, I believe we will see a new weight placed on the work ethic values. It's a conclusion that relates to our model and the concept of some sort of hierarchy. The work ethic values are important only to the extent required to maintain a certain level of satisfaction.

Actually, we should be pleased to see less emphasis on the work ethic, because with the persistence of affluence it means we now have the opportunity to move up a level in the hierarchy of human values. Furthermore, we might even say that work ethic values take on a quality of functional autonomy. They become important for their own sake. Today, it may be healthier to perceive work values as instrumental toward a goal on a particular level than as an all-important reason for life.

As long as our affluence lasts, our work values will be only one set of values among others. Affluence and success have always been factors in reducing drive levels on the work ethic dimension, just as their counterparts, scarcity and failure, have been factors in increasing those drive levels. The wide swings from affluence and success to scarcity and failure have ruined societies and cultures in the past. Some have never recovered their work ethic values, and some never had them to begin with.

The only hope our society has for developing a self-regulation of work values is to develop other values. When affluence and success result from high levels of work values, the work values have done their job. Without replacements, the people become lost, and as has happened in the past, what they have achieved soon withers from lack of proper attention. A set of additive values would, under conditions of affluence, give work values a place but would also provide new values and new goals.

Recognizing and encouraging these new values is something our organizations have not done. They have felt too threatened. They saw the decline in the work ethic as their undoing. In fact, their failure to attend to the emerging value systems has been the real threat. It has left them high and dry. It has made them, at least partially, irrelevant to the needs of their employees. And they wonder why their people aren't motivated? They're not talking to them on their need-level channel any longer.

The prescription for the organization is sensitivity. Pragmatically, this sensitivity must develop from a profit perspective if top management is going to sit up and take notice. Perhaps the self-regulating nature of the marketplace as it still exists among some industries is a good analogy. As the feedback from sales efforts is evaluated, changes in corporate strategy result. As consumer factors in the marketplace change, corporate strategy changes. Nowhere has the need for this market sensitivity been more pronounced than in automobile sales. In this case, American manufacturers had their market eroded by nearly 30 percent before they got the message that the small, well-built car was, temporarily, what the consumer wanted.

This kind of sensitivity, again developing from the profit perspective, has also become a part of labor relations. However slowly our organizations responded to union-management roles, they have now recognized their importance and have developed feedback mechanisms that are permanent systems.

As they did with the marketplace and labor relations, our organizations must develop a system of sensitivity toward human motivation. I believe efforts have been made. The first step is to incorporate into the philosophy of every manager the belief that understanding human behavior is as important to management as is accounting, production, engineering, or marketing. Many managers are now aware of this. However, for every forward step toward understanding, they take two sideways. This is caused by misinformation, misunderstanding, and being misled. The reams of popular literature on the work ethic contribute to this problem.

Managers and organizations aren't sure what the value trends are anymore. Is the work ethic dead or alive? If it's alive, should we increase it? If it's dead, should we try to resurrect it? These issues become misunderstood, in my view, because the manager has never been given the proper tools of evaluation in terms of human behavior. We would not expect a manager to work on problems of finance without some knowledge of the principles of accounting, and yet for too long managers have worked on people problems without knowledge of principles of human behavior.

Broad-Based Limitations

Some of our organizational problems may stem from unrealistic expectations about the structure of the organization. In terms of satisfaction with life, most of us realize the limits of material goods. They do not provide for the more esthetic enrichments of life. However, is it realistic to assume that organized production can satisfy intangible needs such as beauty, truth, and calm? These represent the existential limits of life. They may be no less important than material satisfactions, but are they within the role of the organization?

Without going into a prolonged debate on the role of the organization (we can leave that to Peter Drucker) it is clear that benefiting the individual is only one of the responsibilities of a company. It has others that are of necessity self-serving. We might view this situation as a utilization-equity balance. It is the organizational equivalent of the principle of distributive justice.

Utilization	Equity
What value the company gets from an employee.	What value an employee gets from the company.

There exists a trade-off in this relationship. It takes the form of an overlapping set of self-interests. To the extent that they overlap, they become mutual interests, but to the extent that they do not overlap, they remain separate interests. Thus, there is an area of concern that is solely the company's, and an area that is solely the individual's. To say that the company's interest is the same as the individual's ignores the limitations of this overlap.

From this perspective, it is easy to see that there will be times when each group will be lobbying only for its own interests, and these may be irrelevant or opposed to the interests of the other party. In some instances we might say that on the equity side, the employee's expectations of value from the company were unrealistic. The organization could not, nor should it be expected to, be the total source of value to the individual. This is the myth of the corporate state.

On the utilization side of the scale, the organization cannot fairly expect 100 percent of the employee's life. There must be limits to effort, loyalty, and, yes, even performance. The limits are directly related to the limits of equity, or so they should be. If you, as an employee, do not get all of life's satisfactions from the company, it should not expect a total commitment from you. The point is that the utilization-equity scale is far from being in balance within our society today, yet many people don't even see the scale, let alone the requirements for balancing it.

Balance must rest with the trade-off process. There must be a point for both sides where they say, "This is as far as our mutual interest goes. We can trade no further." For example, let's take an issue like efficiency. If the organization expected the extreme value contribution there, the employee in turn might expect compensation that would put him in the country club bracket. Yet through trade-offs, we come up with the idea of a "fair day's work for a fair day's pay."

Where there is a mutually agreed upon point of balance on this scale, we have not maximized the interests of the company or the individual, but have reached a compromise that is workable, if not ideal, for both. However, the failure of either side to recognize the nature of such a compromise, that is, the limits of satisfaction, results in unrealistic and unattainable expectations. Thus, it is not their motivations that are unrealistic. What is unrealistic is to assume that the satisfaction of these motives rests with the organizational structure or the input of the individual.

For the most part, companies hire adults. Inherently, regarding motivation, this is a major limitation. No modern psychologist would discount the importance of developmental experiences in forming adult motives. In this developmental process, organizations such as schools, churches, and media structures all play a role. But there are other significant influences—family, individual, and cultural influences—over which organizations do not exert direct control.

As a manager, you know that no employee is an untouched, pure example of human motivation. We all carry a good deal of excess baggage with us from our past. Don't underestimate its influence on present behavior. You as a manager, and even your organization, are not responsible for developing, shaping, and satisfying the human race. Ideally, you know what you can do and what is beyond your power and role. Certainly, within these limits there is room for constructive action, but let us not pretend that the possibilities are unlimited.

There are experiences and traits within an individual which no organizational structure or managerial philosophy will change. There are those who believe that one organization may be attempting that role: our government. There is much it can do to influence the experiences of our children organizationally, but individually its influence is compromised. I personally do not believe that there is a simple formula that as our society improves so does human behavior. The interaction is much more complex and beyond the concerns of the manager, so let us accept the limitation for the present and concentrate our efforts on doing what we can within such a proper perspective.

The Problem of Advancement

There seems to be a relationship between our level of motivation and our time perspective. The more we feel a sense of urgency about time, the more intense our desire toward action. A real change in our society may involve our attitude toward time.

There are some deep philosophical roots to our perception of time. Some philosophical psychologists believe that without the awareness of death there would be very little motivation. If this sounds a bit off-the-wall, imagine in your own situation what your drive level would be if hypothetically your average life expectancy was not 70 years, but, say, 200 years. Would you be quite so concerned about that 20-year mortgage on your house, or the fact that you've been at the same job level for two years?

As our ideas about death have changed, so have our motivations toward life changed. Some observers say that the decline of religious dogma has altered our concept of death. Others say that for our young people, being raised under the atomic threat of total annihilation, a sense of living for the present has developed.

Many people today are no longer motivated by futuristic goals. They do not wish to postpone their satisfaction. Whatever opinion you may have of such a here-and-now mentality, you as a manager are faced with employees who feel this way. In fact, you may feel it yourself.

Much of this feeling is a backlash from the preoccupation with vertical movement up a set of priorities. This concern often blocked or prevented enjoyment of the present. This also led us to the assumption that progressive vertical movement was positively valued.

Well, how do we deal with this change in time perspective, and in corresponding motivations against vertical progress? We resort to functional autonomy. Here is the strategy: Instead of attempting to shape and reinforce vertical movement, and to advocate seeking ever and ever higher-level goals, let us encourage a standard of excellence on one level at a time.

For example, suppose you have an employee who is an equipment mechanic but you believe he has the potential to be a good engineer. You call him into your office and ask him about his future plans for personal growth. He says he's happy being a mechanic. Now, you may want to lecture him on the virtues of higher values in an effort to inspire him to actualize more of his potential. In some cases this approach may work quite well, but with many employees who have this new sense of time perspective your pleas will fall on deaf ears.

An alternative approach would be to allow for this new philosophy, and to use the process of functional autonomy. Instead of attempting vertical movement, as such, which would imply the imposition of your values on someone else in terms of what is and what is not an appropriately dignified occupation, you might do better to encourage a standard of excellence at the particular level the employee is already on. How does functional autonomy come in? Well, the effort and behavior that go into achieving a first-rate performance may become internalized. Once this striving is internalized, it has a much better chance of being transferred to different levels.

Thus, you might encourage your employee to be the best mechanic he is capable of being. After he attains a high level of proficiency as a mechanic, the effort that went into it may transfer to another level more easily, and even if it doesn't, the worst you're stuck with is a very good mechanic.

In our preoccupation with advancement, we have often overlooked this standard of excellence on any given level. After an employee has performed with a minimal degree of competence, his next response is, "Now what?" Our answer is to hold out the incentive of vertical movement instead of qualitative horizontal movement. Our whole society has been geared this way, and if there is a trend away from the "advancement-time urgency" mentality it may be to our benefit.

The tragedy here is not to be in what someone else considers a second-rate job. The tragedy is to turn in a second-rate performance and believe that it is first-rate.

The New Role of Participation

We have in recent years heard a great deal about participative management, and it is, at times, difficult to evaluate its motivational impact. Critics of participation say that it alone does not insure the quality of the effort; that is, the quality of effort remains dependent on the usual factors. Furthermore, they say we have been misled into thinking that participation would lead to better decisions.

Some critics maintain that participation is an abdication of a leader's responsibility, that it in effect turns the company over to the employees, and that group decision making is clumsy and inefficient. We are then flung with full force into a meritocracy-versus-democracy controversy, with the disadvantages of participation surfacing.

Many of these disadvantages come from a participatory system that is badly managed. To see the advantages of participation to motivation and performance, we must look at a well-managed example. The system of General Motors' Inland Division fits this requirement.[1]

For nearly 10 years, Inland's 600 line managers have been operating on a participatory management system. Thomas Mathues, the general manager, and most of his managers assert that the system allows them to respond more quickly to annual model changes, and provides the managers with a broader and more varied set of experiences. Here is how their approach is structured:

Teams of 25 to 75 members operate as individual companies and are responsible for one or more product lines.

Team chiefs are specialists in manufacturing, engineering, and so on. Leadership is rotational, with each chief serving four months each year, when the product cycle demands his talents.

A nine-member staff acts as a "board of directors" for each of the teams, reviewing progress at quarterly meetings. The general manager serves as "chairman."

The teams have a wide range of operating discretion so long as they meet their objectives. The whole idea of the teams has

[1]"GM's Test of Participation," *Business Week*, February 23, 1976.

been to break up the little empires that develop and often work at cross-purposes. As one manager put it, "Before the teams, a guy would say, 'I'm the quality control inspector and I don't give a damn about your production problems.' Now all of us are working on common problems."

All team members have access to information necessary for their general management efforts, such as selling prices and materials costs for their product. In fact, based on such data, each team makes up its own operating budget and profits are "loaned" or "borrowed" for capital investment.

What have the bottom line results been? The general management board of directors says that sales in constant dollars (allowing for inflation) increased 45 percent per employee, and 20 percent per square foot of plant space.

Motivational advantages include the fact that even new managers have high visibility. As the general manager observes: "A young engineer two years out of college will be shoved on stage to make a technical presentation because the older engineers may not explain it as well. The team approach allows a young person to show talent earlier." A 30-year-old engineering superintendent agrees. "I hadn't been here a year the first time I stood up before the general manager and told him about our problems. In all eight years with another company, I only saw the general manager once."

Inland management believes that a major advantage of teams is the mobility it offers young employees. It believes there has been considerably more movement between various types of jobs than before the team system.

Inland has had a problem in trying to expand the system, as it exists, to hourly employees. In terms of what we've discussed about motivation, it's easy to see why. For example, maybe Fred doesn't have anything to contribute. Placing him in such a system will only make him feel pressured and threatened. He may not feel that participation is anywhere near his need levels and thus may not even want to contribute in this way. To a person without speaking skills and verbal and conceptual abilities, such a prospect is not at all attractive.

In perspective, a participatory system like Inland's holds promise for educated and aggressive young management, but it meets the needs of only these levels. In order for it to apply to others in an organization, radical changes in the system must occur. Furthermore, in this example, no lessening of accountability and standards of performance has developed from the participation. In fact, individual contributions have increased or decreased on the basis of special technical problems and the special abilities of the personnel. This matching has effectively addressed and eliminated the meritocracy-versus-democracy problem.

This must be the new role of participation: matching the needs and talents of the individual with the requirements of the organization in such a way as to provide a meaningful involvement for both parties. Without overstating the value of participation, we may even say that this combination has the potential to restore an entrepreneurial spirit to management. Thus, a motivational problem of the recent past will be eliminated in the managers of the future. The key to success is *proper implementation* for a good fit or match between person and organization.

A Motivational Cycle

It seems reasonable to assume that, over time, motivation is not constant, nor is it maintained at a consistent level. This is, of course, particularly true for esteem, praise, status, recognition, or love. Therefore, it is unreasonable to assume any motivation that translates into productivity will be constant. Individual productivity varies over time.

We may make reference to this cycle from a fundamental biological concept such as homeostasis, which is a state of balance or equilibrium. The body constantly seeks this state of balance. When the equilibrium is upset by forces of imbalance, a new balance is formed. This repetitive process provides the basis for cyclical fluctuations of the body. The effects on biological motivation are clear. You eat, you get hungry, you eat again. In each case your behavior changes as your bodily needs change. This also occurs when we deal with psychological needs.

To believe that an employee's need for self-esteem is the same no matter what day it is, what the situation is, or how he feels, is to discount the role of this motivational cycle. Additionally, for a manager to force cycle changes may be difficult at the very best, and a waste of effort or counterproductive at worst.

Perhaps an employee has a right not to be motivated all the time. There is some merit to the idea that managerial efforts should be sensitive to the varying need levels, and should be synchronized with such cycles in mind. This may sound too complex for a manager to get involved with, but we all are sensitive to this to one degree or another.

Every manager knows that there are good times and bad times to approach employees. You certainly know this is the case with your boss. In both instances, if you have any political sense at all, you work around these variations, or you wait them out, or you may change your approach. We are talking not only about mood swings in this cycle, but also about the time-out phases of life.

We all feel the need from time to time to go from high gear into first or neutral in order to assess the effect of our efforts and even to savor the rewards of our labor. Again, despite all the talk about a motivational crisis and a decline in the work ethic, a balanced perspective calls for caution against too much motivation, or motivation that is counterproductive. This is evident in the workaholic.

Sometimes, constant drive produces stress. The leading cause of death in this country is cardiovascular problems. A major cause of heart and circulatory problems is hypertension, 70 percent of which is stress related. Thus, managers should be sensitive not only to the presence of a motivational cycle for functional reasons, but to their own cycle for health reasons.

The kind of awareness that we've been referring to can take many forms. One type of cycle is illustrated by the balance theory of change proposed by Kurt Lewin. The first step is called *unfreezing*, which is the awareness and development of the need to change. The second step, *moving*, is a diagnosis of the situation and the establishment of an action plan. The third and last step, *refreezing*, is the evaluation and stabilization of the change.

Knowing when and where employees are in this cycle on any given issue will tell you how receptive motivationally they will be toward your efforts to change their behavior. For instance, you would not spend your time on unfreezing if that phase were already present and it was a moving phase that needed your attention.

From a personal perspective, understanding your own cycle will also allow you to plan your area of concentration. It may also give you new insights into your own behavior. It is difficult for us to see these cycles as they are presently occurring, and often only afterward do we see our behavior clearly, so we need all the present understanding we can get. As Kierkegaard said, "Life can only be understood backwards, but it must be lived forwards."

The System Itself

There are times when I look around the student lounge at the college where I teach, and I ask myself, What are these people going to do in the next ten years? The fact is, I don't know. Are there going to be enough jobs, enough career occupations to develop these college-educated people into motivated and satisfied contributors to our society? What has caused our system to go from an independent, entrepreneurial, encouraging environment to one that fosters a welfare-dependency mentality?

Dr. Charles Hamilton of Columbia University, discussing his research in the black community, said he feels our system does not help because it has developed an inertia that is difficult to end even if we recognize it. For example, there are now black families in Harlem that are fourth-generation welfare recipients. Dr. Hamilton told me these people are simply conduits for the system. His researchers have calculated that it takes an average of *six hours* for a welfare recipient in Harlem to spend *80 percent* of his monthly in-the-pocket allotment. That's a conduit!

Furthermore, most of the agencies set up to coordinate and monitor our social systems spend much of their time trying to get refunded for the next year. The danger here is that such practices have been advanced not only in government but in the private sector as well.

Keep in mind, I am not promoting a racist or reactionary attitude; rather I am pointing out the difference between self-development and survival of the fittest. There is no question that our social structures were proposed to avoid exploitation of the weak and poor by the strong and privileged, but has the system, by its very nature, promoted a decline in motivation for self-development?

Our technical and social structures may have gotten out of control because of our attitudes toward self-indulgence and resignation. As Lewis Mumford points out, this may have locked us into an inertia that we do not wish to change:

> . . . the central problem of technics must be restated: It is that of creating human beings capable of understanding their own nature sufficiently to control, and when necessary to suppress, the forces and mechanisms that they have brought into existence.

> But first we must dig deeper into our innermost being to discover the basis for these coercive promptings. We must ask ourselves: Why does every permission turn into a compulsion? Why is the secret motto of our power-oriented society not just "You can, therefore you may," but, "You may, therefore you must." Is that the new freedom science once promised?[2]

[2]*The Pentagon of Power: The Myth of the Machine,* New York, Harcourt Brace Jovanovich, 1970, p. 187.

Mumford goes on to state that the dependency attitude has led us to believe that the needs of our humanity can be fulfilled solely through our systems. He calls this "the myth of the machine." We have relinquished our responsibility for the human condition to our technical and social systems.

The growth and development of our organizations are directly related to the growth and development of the people who work in them. They shape the system, but let us remember, the system, once created, shapes them.

In order for our organizations to survive, we must understand individual and system limitations and opportunities. We must also be able to integrate this understanding into a framework and policy for action. If we can do it, there is cause for optimism. We will see a new age of human development. If we cannot, we will see a regression of human development, with our technology making us victims of our own design. It is fair to say that we are on a threshold of either outcome.

I don't believe a resolution will come without pain and difficulty. Many will feel lost, overtaken, and alienated. The old management attitudes must be sorted out. What fits and works will stay; what does not must be changed. You, the manager, cannot bury your head and hope that everything will come out satisfactorily.

If you pay lip service to the need for adapting and challenging our systems without getting involved yourself, you may be convinced of your participation, but it will be an illusion. As Adlai Stevenson once said, "It is often easier to fight for principles than to live up to them."

What Should We Do?

Of course, no one answer to the problems of our organizations and society could ever be sufficient to deal with an involved and changing world. One set of guidelines that might help relates to attitudes about people and about life.

1. Accepting humanness. We must first believe that people

are important, that a person is a whole organism, not just a servomechanism that turns out production. We must believe that it is worthwhile to experience life, and that stimulation and zest come from our drive for whatever life has to offer.

2. Understanding human behavior. Awareness of how people behave is our most valuable asset in accepting humanness. To understand is not always to accept, but to accept without understanding is blindness. Only when we know what people need and want can we ever hope to change our lives.

3. Understanding technology. We must never forget the benefits of technology, and yet let us never again hold it out as the panacea for the human condition. We must in the years ahead mature in our attitudes toward the role of technology. We are coming off a very strong intoxication with the power of technics.

4. Being pragmatic. We should not expect too much from our contribution. We are part of that "from many one" that makes up a country or an organization. We must be able to accept our role as only one small part without feeling that the importance of that role is diminished.

5. Being idealistic. We need to have some confidence in people. In their ability to adapt and cope lies the tremendous strength of the human spirit. We must be able to sacrifice now for what we might become.

As a final statement of philosophy on the struggle between the individual and society, we must resort to morality. The question, in its broadest perspective, is that basic. Alan Wheelis's comments in *The Moralist* summarize the situation of choice:

> Nature is amoral; morality is unnatural. Our lives are meridian to these poles. Love and hate, nurture and murder, they spring from our nature with equal authenticity. But nature no longer leads, authenticates nothing. We say love is right and hate is wrong, and so leave nature, struggle toward a moral order.

We live in a jungle and we live in a community. He who would assert either to the exclusion of the other will find ample evidence for the realm of his choice. We know both, but assert that the way of love, of community, of caring for one's neighbor is right, and that the way of the jungle is wrong. No one leads us. We stand aside from nature, seek a god in the image of what we arbitrarily designate as our better selves.[3]

[3]New York, Basic Books, 1973, p. 92.

12
Conclusion:
Now What?

IT has always been my feeling that if an author hasn't said what is most important in a book before the last chapter, it's too late; the reader has already put the book aside. If the major ideas have been presented, then there is no point in restating them. About the only purpose of a concluding chapter is to synthesize and tie in some loose ends and make a number of predictive observations. This is my purpose here.

The Process of Evolution

In the interest of pragmatism, the question of what effect knowledge has on behavior is legitimate. Most readers may remember and *use* only 10 percent of what's been presented in this book. That may sound like an unsuccessful result, but actually it may be quite realistic. The steps from concept to training to practice do not involve a revolutionary process. The process occurs gradually (if at all), making it evolutionary.

You, as a manager, will not use every concept presented here in every problem situation you encounter. You must pick and choose just as in the Situational Principles cases. If you asked me to restate any points that are of particular significance in our evolutionary process, my choice would be these:

1. The concept of functional autonomy. It provides that crucial link between extrinsically and intrinsically directed behavior.

2. The techniques of behavioral engineering. The awareness of behavioral contingency effects takes much of human behavior out of the closet and makes it understandable and manageable.

An effort to incorporate just these two concepts may be so evolutionary as to be generational. I can hear today's managers asking the question, How do I plug it in? The question itself is revealing of the newness of the ideas. You wouldn't ask how you learned to be a pleasant person. Why not? Because it is either an incorporated part of you or it isn't. It's part of your training as an individual—your role perceptions. This is the same with the ideas we've discussed. They must become a part of our lives almost in a cultural sense. Then we will see clearly the evolutionary change.

Why Organizations?

The organizational environment is one of the most atmospheric entities in our world. It shapes values, attitudes, moral and ethical judgments, and cultural norms—all by its selective use of rewards and punishments. It is all-encompassing because of its functional effect; it has given us our civilization. In addition, we are also recognizing that it is a social laboratory filled with human interactions in a concentrated and controlled setting.

Through organizations, we as a people can achieve a mastery not only over our environment, but over ourselves as well. The reason is that organizations are synergistic—that is, the total effect of an organization is greater than the sum of its parts. In other words, organizationally, $2 + 2 = 5$. This is what makes concerted group effort toward a goal so effective, and we are only touching the tip of the iceberg in our understanding of organizational dynamics.

For years, we have recognized that technologies are synergistic. This tended to overshadow what early civilizations knew before technological development: *Persons are also synergistic.* This is the potential lying just beneath the surface in human resource development.

Furthermore, organizations, like people, form a Gestalt. You will recall that at the outset, this book warned of the pitfalls of fragmentation. This is what a Gestalt is all about. It means simply that an individual is so *integrated as a unit* that the unit is different from the sum of its parts. Thus, studying personality traits and adding them up will not give you the interactions that are unique to the whole person.

What I'm getting at, then, is that people and organizations have two important additive dimensions—a quantitative element known as "synergism," and a qualitative element known as "a Gestalt." This is a benefit in general, but, specifically, it makes understanding of the interactions very difficult and complex, and the manager's role is right in the middle.

In this regard, perhaps the importance of the managerial function has been underestimated. I believe it has. We train and develop managers for technical competence, not organizational impact. In that context, personalities take a back seat to other considerations. Are we then to guess at managers' personalities? To me, this seems a bit backward. To imply that a manager is one thing and a person is another is to make too artificial a distinction. Where in our society can a manager go for technical training and guidance as a person? Certainly not within our organizations.

If our institutions are to advance the effect of synergism and Gestalt, they must respond to this oversight. Technically effective programs must be developed. There must be a results-oriented philosophy; and encounter groups, transactional analysis, and transcendental meditation are not going to do the job. In fact, they often produce a backlash toward dehumanization. What is needed, in the broadest sense, is what I said at the outset—a technology of behavior. It must, however, be not a mechanistic technology, but a balanced technology combining the intrinsic worth of the individual with the extrinsic environment. I hope this book has made a contribution toward that balanced technology.

Index